THE REAL MAN'S
GUIDE TO
FIXIN' STUFF

HOW TO REPAIR ANYTHING YOU NEED
(or Just Want) TO KNOW HOW TO FIX

D0010969

THE REAL MAN'S

GUIDE TO

FiXiN' STUFF

HOW TO REPAIR ANYTHING YOU NEED
(or Just Want) TO KNOW HOW TO FIX

NICK HARPER

sourcebooks

Published by Sourcebooks, Inc.
P.O. Box 4410, Naperville, Illinois 60567-4410
(630) 961-3900
Fax: (630) 961-2168
www.sourcebooks.com

Originally published in 2009 in Great Britain by Michael O'Mara Books Limited

Library of Congress Cataloging-in-Publication Data

4430 0746   8/10

Harper, Nick
  The real man's guide to fixin' stuff : how to repair anything you need (or just want) to know how
to fix / by Nick Harper.
     p. cm.
1. Repairing--Amateurs' manuals. 2. Dwellings--Maintenance and repair--Amateurs' manuals.
3. Household appliances--Maintenance and repair--Amateurs' manuals. 4. Do-it-yourself work.
I. Title.
  TH4817.3.H37 2010
  643'.7--dc22
                                  2010001456

                Printed and bound in the United States of America.
                  VP 10 9 8 7 6 5 4 3 2 1

CONTENTS

Acknowledgments   *xi*

Introduction   *xii*

Basic Toolkit   *xiii*

Section 1. Keeping Up Appearances

How to... Fix a Hole in Your Shoe   2

How to... Re-sole Shoes   3

How to... Fix a Broken Heel
(on a Flat, Manly Shoe)   4

How to... Fix a Broken High Heel
(on a Thin, Pointy, Womanly Shoe)   6

How to... Salvage Shrunken Clothes   9

How to... Save Color-Stained White Clothes   10

How to... Remove Common Stains from Clothes   11

How to... Fix Clothing Conundrums   16

How to... Fix Torn Clothes   17

How to... Fix a Run in Tights   18

How to... Patch a Hole in Jeans   19

How to... Prevent Moth Holes in Clothes
(and Exterminate Moths)   20

How to... Fix Holes in Pant/Coat Pockets   22

How to... Fix a Misaligned Zipper   25

How to... Fix a Snapped Handbag/Manbag Strap   26

How to... Fix a Broken Umbrella Stem   27

How to... Fix a Broken Umbrella Spoke   29

How to... Fix Tarnished Jewelry 31

How to... Repair a Broken Wristwatch Strap 32

How to... Fix a Scratched Watch Face 33

How to... Fix Scratched Sunglasses 34

Section 2. Everyday Electrical Stuff

How to... Fix a Television 37

How to... Fix a Remote Control 40

How to... Troubleshoot a Digital Camera 42

How to... Fix a Faulty Cell Phone 45

How to... Troubleshoot a Faulty Telephone 48

How to... Clean a Scratched Disc (CD or DVD) 50

How to... Clean a CD or DVD Player 52

How to... Fix a Faulty Vinyl Record 54

How to... Troubleshoot a Video Player 56

How to... Troubleshoot a Computer 60

How to... Clean a Mouse 62

How to... Fix a Broken Key on a Computer 63

How to... Boost FM Radio Reception 65

How to... Make a Vacuum Cleaner Suck Up More 66

Section 3. White Goods (Big and Small)

How to... Fix a Kettle 70

How to... Mend a Malfunctioning
Microwave Oven 71

How to... Sharpen Blender Blades 76

How to... Troubleshoot Your Toaster 78

How to... Fix a Leaking Washing Machine 80

How to... Kickstart an Underperforming Washing
     Machine   82
How to... Fix a Noisy Washing Machine   83
How to... Fix a Washing Machine Door That
     Won't Open   84
How to... Fix an Underperforming Dishwasher   85
How to... Fix a Faulty Refrigerator   86
How to... Fix a Leaking Refrigerator   89
How to... Fix a Faulty Freezer   92

Section 4. Kitchen Conundrums

How to... Fix a Broken Plate   96
How to... Fix a Broken Cup Handle   101
How to... Fix a Broken Glass Stem   102
How to... Sharpen Blunt Kitchen Knives
     (the Professional Way)   104
How to... Sharpen a Can Opener   106
How to... Sharpen Scissors   106
How to... Make Knives and Forks Sparkle
     Like New   108
How to... Resuscitate a Battered
     Chopping Board   109
How to... Fix a Burnt Pan   111
How to... Blitz Rust on a Cast-Iron Pan   112
How to... Fix Rusty Baking Dishes   114

Section 5. Fixtures, Furniture, and Furnishings

How to... Fix a Squeaking Bed   116
How to... Fix a Wobbly Chair or Table   117

How to... Fix Squeaky Stairs 119

How to... Fix Creaking Floorboards 120

How to... Bleed a Radiator 122

How to... Fix Stuck Drawers: Part I 124

How to... Fix Stuck Drawers: Part II 125

How to... Fix a Squeaking Door 125

How to... Fix Loose Door Hinges 126

How to... Fix a Loose Doorknob 128

How to... Fix a Sticking Lock 129

How to... Fix Scratched Windows 130

How to... Fill a Gouge in Wooden Furniture 131

How to... Fix Blistering Paint 133

How to... Repair Damaged Plaster 135

How to... Eradicate Carpet Stains 136

How to... Save an Ailing Carpet 140

Section 6. Bathroom Business

How to... Unblock a Toilet 144

How to... Fix a Toilet That Won't Flush 145

How to... Fix a Dripping Tap 148

How to... Fix a Tap That Won't Turn 151

How to... Unblock Clogged Sinks 152

How to... Fix a Trickling Shower 154

How to... Fix a Leaking Shower 156

How to... Fix a Cracked Bath 157

How to... Fix a Cracked Bathroom Tile 159

Section 7. Garden Guidance

How to... Fix a Sagging Garden Gate   162
How to... Fix a Blocked Gutter   164
How to... Sharpen Garden Tools   166
How to... Rescue Rusting Tools   169
How to... Troubleshoot a Faulty Electric Mower 170
How to... Fix a Cracked Flower Pot   174
How to... Piece Together a Broken Plant Pot 177
How to... Fix a Torn Garden Umbrella   178
How to... Repair a Hose With a Hole   179

Section 8. Sports and Leisurely Pursuits

How to... Fix Books   182
How to... Fix a Fishing Rod   186
How to... Fix a Sluggish Skateboard   187
How to... Replace the Tip of a Pool/Snooker Cue 189
How to... Re-Grip a Tennis/Badminton Racket 190
How to... Re-Grip a Golf Club   192
How to... Adjust Bicycle Brakes: Part I   193
How to... Adjust Bicycle Brakes: Part II   196
How to... Replace Worn Brake Blocks   197
How to... Patch Up a Bicycle Puncture   198
How to... Repair a Scratched Car   201
How to... Fix a Defective Windshield Wiper   203
How to... Fix a Flat Tire   205

To Sarah, Lou, and Jim

ACKNOWLEDGMENTS

Big thanks to all at Michael O'Mara, most notably Hannah Knowles for her patient editing in the face of nonsensical instructions, and Toby Buchan, Ana Bjezancevic, Ana Sampson, and Florence Hallett. Without you all, this book would not exist and people would be staring blankly at the palms of their hands.

INTRODUCTION

Back in the good old days, things were made properly, pieced together with pride. Now, however, everything's put together on conveyor belts by robots (probably) and you're lucky if it lasts six months before breaking down on you. You don't complain though, do you? No, you just throw it away and buy a new one. And when that breaks in six months' time, you throw that away and buy a new one. And when that breaks, the sorry cycle continues: The manufacturer gets richer, you get poorer, and the giant landfill gets ever higher; it's a terrible business.

Some people take a stand and call out "a man" to fix it for them for vast amounts of cash. But there is a simple alternative: The next time a household item breaks down, (and it will, make no mistake) simply set about fixing it yourself. We're not talking any of the complicated stuff that might kill you—like stripping down the boiler or any fiddly rewiring jobs around the house—stuff like that is best left to the experts. We mean the simple things in life: the dripping tap, torn pants, bike brake problems—simple things that any one of us could fix with just a small box of tools, a dollop of common sense, and some clear instructions.

Now *The Real Man's Guide to Fixin' Stuff* cannot provide you with any tools or common sense, but it can provide the clear instructions for most things. Starting over the page, and not before time, help is finally at hand...

BASIC TOOLKIT

Allen key Mini wrench for tightening/loosening screws with recessed internal-hexagon heads.

Chisel Handheld tool with sharp-edged end, designed to cut into materials such as wood and metal.

Drill Makes light work of drilling holes of various sizes in wood and what have you. Electric drills are available very cheaply at DIY stores.

Files Hand tool used to shape materials by filing away until they reach the desired dimensions. A basic hand file should suffice for most purposes.

Hacksaw Fine-tooth saw that both saws and kind of hacks at the material you're working on. A lightweight alternative to a real saw.

Hammer Essential bludgeoning implement for knocking nails into wood.

Nails Keep a good supply of these, in varying lengths and models.

Needle and thread Carry a mini sewing kit on you at all times; you'll be surprised how often it comes in handy.

Plunger Big wooden handle with a rubber head, invaluable for unblocking sinks and the toilet.

Pliers Snappy little hand tool designed to pinch and hold objects, cut wires and bend things into new shapes—gripping pliers are best for everyday fixes.

Sandpaper Abrasive paper designed to smooth surfaces. Graded in various "grits" (level of abrasiveness). Buy a selection, just to be on the safe side.

Saw Cuts through wood and similar materials with indecent haste, providing you've invested in a saw with sharp, angry teeth.

Screwdriver This screw tightener/loosener is available with various screw heads, but the most useful are the "flathead" and the "crosshead" Phillips.

Screws Available in numerous sizes, shapes, materials, and models, you'll need to invest in a good selection so that you have the right screw for the job.

Spirit level Instrument designed to determine when surfaces are level, which is useful for leveling up wonky tables and shelves.

Utility knife Also known as a carpet/stationary/Stanley knife. Take care when cutting, as the replaceable blade should be devastatingly sharp.

Vise A mechanical clamp used to hold things—wood usually—perfectly still while you saw/hack them.

Wrench This hand tool takes the effort out of tightening and loosening nuts and bolts. Buy a set with varying head sizes to cover most jobs.

KEEPING UP APPEARANCES

Image is everything, they say, which means it's not socially acceptable to turn up at work or a social gathering in a pair of shoes with the heel hanging off or wearing a tiny sweater that shrunk in the wash and now restricts your breathing. Nor is it the right thing to venture out in frayed, ripped, or moth-eaten clothing, nor tights with runs, nor a shirt or blouse splattered with blood and ketchup stains. No, no, no.

We don't make the rules, but rules are rules and we must all abide by them. So, with your sartorial standing in mind, and to guarantee you make the right impression, we kick off with essential tips on keeping up appearances...

How to... Fix a Hole in Your Shoe

If your shoe is letting in water and you squelch with every step, you probably have a hole in the sole that needs patching up. Here you have two options, depending on the type of hole you have.

Option 1. If it's a hole you could shove your finger through, your best bet is to cut a length of duct tape to size and smooth it out across the hole on both the inside and outside of the shoe. Duct tape is waterproof, of course, which helps keep the water out, plus additional layers can be added if you need to build up the sole. This will provide a temporary fix until you can get home and re-sole the shoe, which is what it needs (details on the following page).

Option 2. If the sole leaks, but there is no obvious hole to speak of, it's more likely that a crack or cracks in the sole are allowing water in. This again is due to shoddy workmanship at the factory, or the fact you've worn the shoes into the ground. Either way, the cracks can easily be fixed. First, invest in a tube of super-strength, waterproof glue or cement, then gently push and pull the shoe's sole until signs of a crack appear. When you find the crack(s), work a good splodge of glue into it, wipe away any excess, and hold the shoe firm until the glue has set. Your shoe should now be waterproof once more.

How to... Re-sole Shoes

This requires proper concentration because you'll be whipping off a defective sole with a knife and replacing it with a new piece you bought earlier. You should only attempt this if the sole has ground right down. So, when you have a replacement sole in the appropriate size and style, available from all good shoe shops, you're ready for what is a fairly simple three-step procedure.

Step 1. Make sure the sole of the shoe is free from any mud or debris and is bone dry, then take a utility (or carpet) knife and **very carefully** cut away the defective sole, either all the way if it's a trainer-type affair, or right up to the heel if it's a more formal affair. When the sole is finally removed, sand the surface of the shoe to remove any old glue, giving it a nice rough finish, then sand the surface of the replacement sole. This should help them adhere more easily when you come to put the new sole on.

Step 2. Unless the new sole is self-adhesive, you'll need to slather a good spread of shoe cement on both the shoe and the new sole. Line the two parts up neatly and push them firmly together. Once the two parts have started to stick, put the shoe on and gently stand in it for a while to encourage a tighter seal.

Step 3. Unless the new sole was an exact match for the shoe, you will probably have a little overhang that will need to be carefully trimmed away with your utility knife, then filed or sanded to a clean finish. Repeat the above on the other shoe, if required, and if you also need to re-heel the shoes then read on.

MINOR REPAIRS

If the sole has merely come loose and can be stuck back into place, pull the sole gently until you're able to squeeze a good splodge of shoe cement into the gap. Push the two parts together, wipe away any excess that leaks out, then apply weight to the shoe to encourage the cement to bond tightly. Let the cement bond fully before using the shoe again.

How to... Fix a Broken Heel (on a Flat, Manly Shoe)

A stupidly simple fix, this. So simple, in fact, it's almost an insult to your intelligence to outline it here, but your heel is broken and you need a fix. If the heel is damaged beyond repair, you'll need to buy a replacement heel from a shoe shop. If it has merely come loose but is otherwise in decent condition, you can re-attach it.

Step 1. Gently pull the loose heel away from the body of the shoe, using a knife for extra leverage if required. Remove any old glue from the surface, then sand that surface so it ends up a little rough. Repeat this on the underside of the heel: Remove any old glue, then sand until it's a little rough so that when you glue the two parts back together they'll bond better.

Step 2. Apply a super-strength waterproof glue to both the surface of the shoe and the replacement heel (or original heel if it's just come loose), press the two parts together and hold them firmly in place until the glue begins to grip. When this happens, put the shoe on and stand in it to encourage it to adhere. Once it's fully dried, you'd be wise to drive a few shoe nails around the perimeter of the heel to secure it. However, make damn sure the nails go through the heel's edge and into the shoe, but not through the heel, through the shoe, and out into the part you plan to stand on. That will cause your feet to bleed and your eyes to water.

Step 3. And that's it. There really is no Step 3, apart from to suggest you repeat this process on the other shoe so that your heels match, though that's entirely optional— and unnecessary if you're re-affixing a good heel that has simply come loose.

How to... Fix a Broken High Heel (on a Thin, Pointy, Womanly Shoe)

Even a pair of fancy-pants shoes with an outrageous price tag can snap at the heel, sending you flying and leaving you in an unladylike heap on the floor. Luckily, quick-fix help is at hand here, though how you react depends on the type of damage done and your surroundings when it happens.

IF THE HEEL BREAKS ON THE HOOF

The wise women amongst you will know to carry a small tube of a tough-wearing, shoe-specific adhesive about their person at all times, allowing them to apply a quick fix in emergencies. This may not provide a long-term solution, but it will at least allow you to get to wherever it is that you're going. When the heel has snapped or hangs off, how the shoe was constructed will determine how you go about mending it.

Option 1. If it's a simple glued-on heel, clean and scrape away any old glue, apply a generous dollop of your fresh glue to the two broken parts—heel and sole—and push them firmly together. Clasp tightly until the glue has dried fully, put the shoe back on your foot, and continue walking to wherever it is you were going.

Option 2. If the heel is attached to the sole with glue and a number of small shoe nails, all of which are still in working order, coat the nail ends with your glue and push them back into their corresponding holes in the heel (see diagram). Hold in place until the glue has dried, then be about your business.

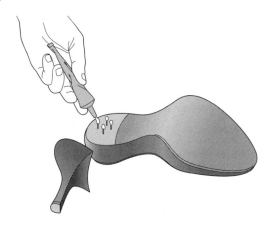

Option 3. If the heel has snapped clean in two, glue the two parts together again and take your chances, but the shoe's stability has been fatally compromised and another clean snap is most likely just a few paces away. You would be better whipping the shoes off and getting a taxi home or to the shoe repair shop.

IF THE HEEL BREAKS AT HOME OR IN THE OFFICE

The technique here is pretty much the same as that detailed above, only your repairs can and should be more thorough. Once again you'll need a tube of sturdy, shoe-specific glue, which you'll use to bond heel and sole back together. Before applying the glue, however, make sure that both parts are dry and free of any old glue. Gently sand the affected areas to ensure a better purchase when you stick the two parts together. But because this is a thin, high heel, you'll need to keep the pressure for at least twenty-four hours to guarantee a firm finish, so creative use of an elastic band or string to secure the parts in place is advisable. Obviously, if the heel is held in place using glue and nails, you'll need to pull out any old nails and drive replacements home into the already-established holes before applying the elastic band or string.

WARNING!

If the heel of your shoe breaks in more than one place, there is no real quick fix. Your best bet would be to replace the whole heel, but this may then necessitate you replacing the heel on the other shoe to ensure a clean match. This is a job best left to a professional shoe repairer, otherwise known as a cobbler. Also, be aware that the heel of a new shoe should not break easily, certainly not as you're walking down the street, minding your own business. If it does, and if you still have the receipt, return the shoe to the shop from whence it came and demand your money back.

How to... Salvage Shrunken Clothes

Before you read the solution, here is a warning: Not all clothing can be salvaged. If it's a delicate material, such as silk or cotton, you will struggle; if it's a more robust wool or cotton sweater that shrunk because you programmed the machine all wrong though, you may be in luck.

Step 1. Place the garment in a sink filled with warm water and leave to soak for fifteen minutes.

Step 2. Remove it and squeeze out the water, then pat it dry with a towel so that the garment is damp. Not wet, not dry, just damp.

Step 3. Finally—and this is the vital part—lay the garment flat on a surface and very carefully stretch it back to something approaching its original shape. This may not work if the garment has shrunk to toddler size, but it represents your last hope.

An alternative approach is to stick the garment on a coat hanger and let the damp weight stretch it back into shape. With this option, however, you have less control over the shape of the garment, so it really depends on your desperation levels.

How to... Save Color-Stained White Clothes

A rogue red sock in a white wash can ruin the whole load, turning all your white clothes a very sorry shade of pink. Rather than fling them all out, try the following as a last resort:

WARNING!

Do not use this fix on silk, spandex, or wool clothing as you will ruin your garment.

Step 1. Submerge the garment in a tub of cold water and add a capful or two of bleach.

Step 2. Leave for five to ten minutes and rinse with cold water.

Step 3. Wash as normal, making certain that the red sock is not inside the washing machine, and cross your fingers.

How to... Remove Common Stains from Clothes

SIX BASIC RULES OF STAIN REMOVAL

1. For the best results you'll need to address the stain as quickly as possible, preferably before it dries.

2. Always check the manufacturer's instructions before undertaking any stain removal and do exactly as it says. If the garment doesn't carry any warning, try Rule 3 below on a section of the clothing you won't see—normally on the inside round the back would be best.

3. Blot the stain rather than rubbing hard and smearing the stain and thereby damaging the fibers. Also, to isolate the stain, only ever work from the outside in.

4. Only when the stain is *completely* eradicated should you iron the area. Heat can set the stain and make removing it much harder.

5. Silk, spandex, and wool clothing should never be bleached—this will cause irreparable damage.

6. After all treatments mentioned here, wash your garments thoroughly as you would normally to remove any stain remover residue.

VARIOUS STAINS...

Ink: A dash of rubbing alcohol should do the trick here, applied as quickly as possible with a soft, clean cloth and then washed as usual. Hairspray also works wonders, providing you allow the spray to penetrate the fabric before washing as usual.

Chewing Gum: This fix only applies to jeans and *never* on delicate fabrics (which will need to be sent to a dry cleaner, sadly). Never pull and scratch at chewing gum; you'll only spread the stain. Instead, freeze it with an ice cube or, better still, by leaving it in a plastic bag in the freezer for a few hours.

When the gum has frozen, gently chip away at it with a blunt knife and dab on an alcohol-based solvent to remove any unsightly residue that you can't chip off.

Wine: Blot with cold water (never hot, as that will make the stain set), then sprinkle salt onto the stain and watch in awe as it soaks up the color. Rinse with water and sponge with rubbing alcohol, then wash as you normally would. (This method also applies to coffee and most tomato-based stains.)

Ketchup & Mustard: Scrape away any excess carefully with a knife; rinse the garment in cold water with mild detergent, working up into a lather with your fingertips. Rinse in cold water, then wash as usual.

Grease: Scrape off excess with a blunt knife and place the stain face down on a paper towel, which should suck up some of the grease. Then, on the underside of the stain, squeeze a small blob of soap and work into a gentle lather with your finger. Finish by washing on the hottest setting the garment can take.

Blood: With fresh blood, simply keep the stain wet and rinse out under the cold water tap. If the blood has dried, soak the garment in salty water overnight, then soak in water with a dash of ammonia and wash as usual.

Chocolate: Taking care not to push it further into the fabric, scrape away as much chocolate as possible with a knife, then rinse the stain thoroughly from the back of the fabric with cold, and preferably sparkling water, working it in gently. Next, rub on a splodge of liquid detergent and leave it on the garment for five to ten minutes before soaking in cold water for fifteen minutes. Then, check the stain and repeat as necessary until the chocolate loosens, lifts, and then disappears completely. If the stain stubbornly remains, add a dash of ammonia to the detergent mix if it was milk chocolate, or two tablespoons of white vinegar for dark chocolate, and rinse again. Then wash as usual.

Lipstick: If you can get it quickly, dab at the stain with a moist paper towel and it should lift nicely. Then rub the stain with Vaseline and wash in hot soapy water to remove the stain completely. If the mark has dried, blot the stain with cold water, then take a cotton ball dipped in ammonia and dab at the stain to lift and remove.

Tea & Coffee: Mix one teaspoon of white vinegar with two pints of cold water, then spray onto the stain and blot. This should loosen and bring the stain out. Then wash as normal.

Grass: Gently dab at the area with rubbing alcohol before washing the garment as usual, although a splodge of soap left to nibble at the stain for fifteen minutes before you wash as normal can also do the job for you here.

Mud: Left to dry, much of the mud can be brushed off into the trash can: Rubbing at a wet mud stain will merely smear it all over the garment. A number of detergent-based solutions would work here, but the best and most inventive fix is to slice a raw potato in half and rub the starchy innards on the stain, then soak the garment in cold water for an hour before washing as normal. Don't eat the potato, but if you do, at least brush off the mud first.

Fruit: Is a nuisance, because the acids can eat into the fabric. So act very fast by sprinkling salt onto the stain before rinsing in cold water. Wash as normal in a liquid detergent containing hydrogen peroxide.

Permanent Marker: The name is the giveaway here and the following advice may not work, but it's worth a shot rather than throwing the garment away. So, rinse the stain with cold water until the water runs clear, then place a paper towel beneath the stain and douse the stain generously with rubbing alcohol, blotting with a soft cloth. As the alcohol takes hold, the color should be drawn out into the paper towels, which will need to be changed as they absorb the ink. When no more ink comes out, wash the garment at the hottest temperature it will take (see label), adding in a dash of bleach, or color-safe bleach for colored fabrics, then rinse in warm water.

How to... Fix Clothing Conundrums

Here are three very quick tips for reviving shabby clothes that you might ordinarily throw away.

Tip 1. Make Colored Clothes Brighter
Colors fade over time, but that's nothing a dash of white vinegar added to your rinse cycle can't remedy in a matter of minutes. The colors should come out more vibrant.

Tip 2. Make White Clothes Whiter
Whites grow grubby the more you wear them, but this can be fixed by soaking the garment in warm water mixed with an oxygen-based bleaching agent (available in the supermarket) for twenty-four hours, then rinsing in a sink full of warm water with a dash of vinegar. Aim for one tablespoon of vinegar for every four cups of water and you should be about right.

Tip 3. Make Black Clothes Blacker
Black clothes lose their intensity and lighten over time, but this can be remedied by adding either one cup of strong coffee or two cups of tea in the rinse cycle, minus the milk and sugar, obviously. When the garment dries, the intensity should be restored. Any lingering whiff of tea or coffee should be gone after one normal wash.

These fixes are safe only on robust, machine-washable clothes, not on delicate items, which should always be fixed by an expert.

How to... Fix Torn Clothes

How you approach this one depends on the severity of the tear and its position on your clothing. Large tears on important items of clothing—let's say a dinner jacket or a posh frock, for example—should be left to a clothes mending service.

However, smaller tears on jeans and sweaters can be fixed fairly easily by you. The simplest way of doing this is to buy a length of iron-on mending tape, available at most decent department stores and olde worlde haberdashers. Opt for the washable type, in a shade that closely matches the garment you're fixing. It's good for patching up most medium- and heavy-weight materials, and crucially, it's a damn sight easier than stitching the tear. To apply, do as follows...

Step 1. Turn the ripped garment inside out and cut the tape to the shape required, adding an extra inch or so on all sides and rounding off the corners.

Step 2. Lay the edges of the tear back together—they need to be clean tears for this to work; if they're too ragged or parts of the garment have ripped clean off, leaving you with a hole, your only option may be to iron on a patch (see page 19).

Step 3. Iron the back of the torn area to preheat it, then lay the tape on the tear, adhesive side down. Iron over it again to bond the tape to the fabric and leave to cool before moving, or wearing, the garment.

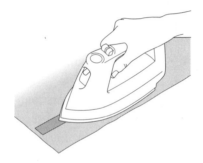

How to... Fix a Run in Tights

This is only a temporary fix and will only work if you catch the run early and act fast, before it races away up your leg. As quickly as possible, apply clear nail polish to the first signs of a hole. When this dries, it will hold the fibers together, keeping the run at bay and buying you some time until you can replace the tights.

How to... Patch a Hole in Jeans*

Acting early is the key here. If you can live with a small hole and don't feel the need to cover it up, just apply glue to arrest the spread (see box below for details).

If you can't live with a small hole, or if the hole is fairly large, the simplest solution is to buy an iron-on denim patch that matches the shade and texture of your jeans. It goes on the inside, so turn the jeans inside out and position the patch over the hole, making sure it's just large enough to cover the hole. Apply moderate heat with an iron to fuse the patch onto the jeans and leave to cool before wearing them again.

*A QUICK FIX FOR SMALL HOLES

If a very small hole or fraying appears in your clothing, trim off any straggly bits, turn the garment inside out, and smear a little waterproof fabric glue around the inside of the hole or edge of the fraying. Leave it to set and once it's hardened, the glue will prevent the hole/fraying from spreading outward and extend the life of your garment.

How to... Prevent Moth Holes in Clothes (and Exterminate Moths)

The only surefire way to prevent moth holes in clothes is to kill every last moth and all moth larvae you can find in your house, although even that may not be possible since they have an uncanny knack of getting into houses through vents and such. Prevention rather than cure is the key here, because once a moth and all his mates go to work on your precious pullover, only an expert will be able to salvage things for you.

So, act early and keep your eyes open for any signs of moth molestation. The following suggestions should help.

Tip 1. Remove any carpet from the bottom of your wardrobe, because this is a breeding ground for the beasties and encourages them to move in.

Tip 2. Never put away clothes that aren't clean; moths are particularly attracted to human sweat. Wear or air clothes as much as possible as moths also dig the dark.

Tip 3. If you do have to leave your clothes hanging unused for months on end in the wardrobe, store them in vacuum-sealed plastic bags between seasons to keep the moths out—the little sods can't survive without air.

Tip 4. Have any clothes you suspect may have come into contact with moths cleaned by a professional, but be sure to mention your moth problem so that they can remove any larvae. Even if you can't see signs of larvae, that doesn't mean there aren't any there.

Tip 5. Wash the clothes at 120°F (50°C) or higher for thirty minutes to kill the moths, or stick clothes that can't be hot-washed in the freezer. This will also terminate their sorry little lives. Bad karma, perhaps, *but the little insects want to eat your sweater!*

Tip 6. Vacuum your clothes cupboards but make certain you empty the bag in the vacuum into an outside trash can straight afterwards; otherwise, the larvae could regroup and grow again.

Tip 7. To truly get rid of moths, you'll need to invest in a reputable moth-killing solution available at most big supermarkets. Or pay a professional man in a full face-mask to fumigate your wardrobe for you.

Tip 8. Finally, once you have eliminated all signs of moths, use cedar, lavender, or dried orange peel to deter them from ever returning. Moths hate all three; however, these deterrents can leave terrible oily stains and damage the fibers of your garments, so make sure they don't come into contact with clothes.

How to... Fix Holes in Pant/Coat Pockets

There are two obvious problems here: Either the seams have come loose and the pocket now flaps around, or there's a hole in the fabric where you've been playing pocket billiards too much. Either way, your money falls out and you'll soon be penniless. Luckily, there are also two very simple fixes.

Option 1. Turn the pant/coat pocket inside out and cut a piece of fabric big enough to cover the hole—aim for half an inch (approx. 1 cm) or so larger than the hole itself. Pin the patch in place with, erm, pins (preferably fabric pins but that's not vital), then stitch the edges together (see box opposite), making sure it's airtight all the way round.

Option 2. The other option is to use a heat-sealing patch instead of sewing. Then you can spend the time you would have spent sewing doing something more interesting, like eating or complaining about the weather. The heat-sealing patch instructions are on pages 17–18.

STITCHED UP

Basic sewing for absolute beginners:

Step 1. Thread the needle by pushing the end of the thread through the eye of the needle, which will take a keen eye and a steady hand. Once through, pull the thread to the desired length—adding a little extra so you don't come up short.

Step 2. Now tie a knot at the end of the thread to keep it securely in place as you sew—then tie a second knot (and sometimes a third if the knot doesn't look large enough to stay secure). Poke the needle through from the underside of the fabric until you feel it catch on the knot at the end, and now you're ready to sew.

Step 3. The easiest stitch is the "running" stitch, which is an evenly spaced straight stitch (see following page). Start close to the knot (which should be on the underside of your fabric) you've just anchored your thread with, and weave the needle in and out of the fabric, keeping the stitches straight and evenly spaced. Avoid long stitches as they are more likely to snag and break, so keep them fairly short.

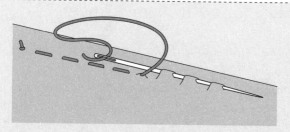

Step 4. When you've stitched the full perimeter of the patch, either go round again for extra security, or anchor the end by taking the needle through to the underside of the garment and looping the thread through the last stitch you made a few times until secure. Then snip and you're done.

Quick-Fix Button Repair

To keep buttons from dropping off your clothes ever again, dab a small drop of clear nail polish onto the thread that secures the buttons. When it dries, it will harden and make it nigh on impossible for thread to weaken and break off.

How to... Fix a Misaligned Zipper

When the teeth of a zipper come apart, zippering your garment up becomes an almighty struggle. However, as long as the teeth of the zipper have simply become misaligned, rather than the whole thing being damaged and needing to be completely replaced, the fix is simple enough.

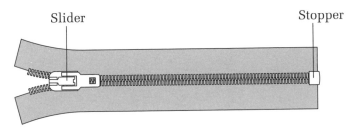

Slider

Stopper

Step 1. Take a pair of pliers and pull off the plastic or metal square stopper at the bottom of the zipper, taking care not to cause any unnecessary damage.

Step 2. Pull the slider all the way down to the bottom, below the two final teeth but not completely off. Now, realign the teeth by hand, making sure they align cleanly from bottom to top. Then, zipper the thing up, marveling at the smooth passage from bottom to top.

Step 3. Now replace the stopper onto the bottom of the zipper by clamping it onto the material on either side of the zipper with pliers. If the stopper's broken, several thick stitches across the bottom of the final two teeth will hold the zipper in place when you take your garment off, providing the stitches are meaty enough. When happy with them, tie a double knot in the thread and snip to finish the job.

How to... Fix a Snapped Handbag/ Manbag Strap

Overfilling your handbag with unnecessary bits and pieces will put a great strain on its straps, a strain that will eventually lead to the seams splitting, the straps snapping, and all your precious belongings crashing out onto the floor.

In future, limit how much you stuff into your bag, avoid swinging it by the handles, and *never* leave it hanging off a doorknob when not in use. Bit late for sage advice now, of course, for you have a bag strap that has snapped and needs fixing. Your task is made far easier if your bag strap is made of canvas, nylon, or some other similarly lightweight material. If so...

Step 1. If the damage is nothing more complicated than a split seam or seams, simply fit the strap back into place, ensuring it will sit at the correct length.

Step 2. Pin the strap into place and sew it back onto the bag along the original seam as neatly as possible, using a stout needle and thread if penetrating the material proves tricky.

Step 3. If the damage is more severe than a damaged seam—let's say the strap has ripped into two pieces, for example—then you may be better off undoing the stitching and sewing on a new strap or straps, or paying an expert to fix it for you.

For a leather bag, follow the same instructions, but your job will be much harder, because running stitches through thick leather is not easy. You may have success using heavy-duty synthetic thread and an equally resilient needle that won't snap at the first sign of resistance. If not, ask your local shoe repair man; he can almost certainly help.

How to... Fix a Broken Umbrella Stem

The stem (the long, thin middle section of the umbrella) holds the full weight of the umbrella and takes a fearsome buffeting in stormy weather, so don't be surprised if it eventually snaps under all the pressure. Never mind, though, because all is not lost.

Option 1. Providing it's a clean break on a one-piece

wooden or plastic stem, an ultra-strong waterproof adhesive slathered onto the snap can often bond both pieces back together, although you will need to apply as many extra layers of glue as possible to provide a strong enough bond, particularly if you live in an area of high winds and thrashing rain.

Option 2. For a far sturdier alternative, drill a small hole lengthways into both parts of the broken stem, then take a dowel of the appropriate size and slather it and the two ends to be joined in wood glue.

Push the dowel into the hole on the handle end of the umbrella, then push the protruding dowel into the hole on the other part of the stem—the dowel should act as a bridge between the two snapped parts and holds them securely. (The holes you've drilled need to be perfectly straight and snug, to accommodate the dowel and ensure no movement.) Finally, for extra security, add a layer of glue around the join, leave it to dry, then apply another layer and leave that to dry, then sand it down to a nice neat finish.

How to... Fix a Broken Umbrella Spoke

One of the most common complaints where umbrellas are concerned is that the spokes will snap in the face of hefty gusts sent down from on high and leave you at the mercy of the damn rain. The spokes shouldn't snap, of course, but as you'll have guessed by now, poor workmanship is often at play here.

Snapped spokes are bad news, because you need them to push up when the umbrella is fully opened and provide support for the canvas and shape for the umbrella as a whole. Each spoke needs to be strong enough to withstand any windy gusts—if it's not, and it snaps, the canvas will blow in on itself and your umbrella will lose all shape, leaving you soaked and irate. Luckily, as with most things, there is a fairly simple solution for this.

A FAIRLY SIMPLE SOLUTION

Gently push at each spoke for signs of weakness—any that are clearly damaged or seem close to breaking will need to be removed. Providing your umbrella features single-piece spokes, each should be held in place at either end by a nubby little bit. Don't be bamboozled by the terminology here—the spoke should just push into place at either end and be held securely. With any damaged spokes, pull out both ends, either by hand or using a pair of pliers if they offer resistance.

To replace the spoke, you'll need to buy a bicycle

spoke of a similar width from your friendly bike shop and cut the length down to the correct size using a hacksaw, then file down and smooth off any angry end points.

Provided the new spoke has a little flexibility about it—as in it bends in the middle—it should be fairly easily inserted into either end and held in place. Your umbrella should once again work as you'd expect it to and you can be about your business.

WARNING!

Sadly, this solution will only work on umbrellas with single-piece spokes, rather than those models with complicated hinge and brackets all over the place. This will be clear when you inspect your umbrella.

HEAVY METAL—AN ALTERNATIVE APPROACH

If the umbrella has a metal stem, glue the two parts together, then wrap a small, thin piece of wire tightly around the join. Secure the stem in a vise, then apply heat to the wire until it begins to melt. The heat should be applied by a cook's blow torch (a proper big blow torch is too dangerous). You're basically soldering here, and when the glue and wire melts, then dries, and covers the snap, it will form a stronger, reinforced bond with the stem and the umbrella will work as good as new.

How to... Fix Tarnished Jewelry

The natural oils in your skin and the manufactured gunk you slather yourself in will eventually leave your jewelry marked and looking really shitty, as they say in the trade. Luckily, reinvigorating most jewelry is a fairly simple task if you follow these rules.

Cleaning Gold*: Soak the gold for fifteen minutes in a bowl of hot soapy water with very mild detergent, then scrub it gently with a soft toothbrush, rinse in lukewarm water, and leave on the side to dry. If the marks are particularly stubborn, use the toothbrush to apply a small splodge of white toothpaste to the stain and work in with a circular motion. Wash clean with soapy water and buff to a sheen with a soft cloth.

Cleaning Silver: When cleaning silver, follow the same procedure as with gold, using toothpaste for stubborn stains. For an advanced finish, apply a liquid silver jewelry cleaner, following the instructions on the packaging.

* If it's white gold it will usually be plated with rhodium, which is a hard, durable, silvery-white metal that can be polished to a high shine but will eventually turn yellowy as the plate wears off. Fixing this will mean having it re-rhodiumed, which is a job best left to a jeweler.

Cleaning Diamonds: Soak the diamonds in warm, soapy water with a very mild detergent (and not, under any circumstances, should you be tempted, chlorine bleach), then scrub gently with a soft toothbrush. Remove from the solution, rinse under lukewarm water, and dry with a soft cloth or leave to dry naturally. For an advanced finish, apply a liquid jewelry cleaner, following the instructions on the packaging. If the diamonds are loose in their setting, consult an expert and have him fix it for you; otherwise, you risk them falling out in the street and rolling into the gutter.

How to... Repair a Broken Wristwatch Strap

Trying to fix all the very fiddly nuts and bolts business inside a watch is a complicated job best left to the experts. However you can take care of the most common watch problem—fixing a broken or damaged strap-yourself. This will only work if it's a metal wrist strap with little pins holding its links in place, and if you've bought a replacement band from a jeweler's before you begin. When you've done so, read on...

Step 1. At the end of the strap, where it hooks onto the watch case, you'll see a small black hole, inside which sits a small pin, with another one on the opposite side. Using a spring bar tool (available from all good jewelers), push into the hole and the pin should pop out the opposite end. Repeat on the other pin.

Step 2. Remove the strap and insert a pin into the holes on the case to push out any grime. Now take your new strap, and position the ends so that when you reinsert the pins they skewer it and hold it in place. Use the spring bar to push the pin in as far as it will go, then secure the other end of the strap in the same way.

Step 3. That's all there is to it, although it's probably worth mentioning that if the strap needs links removing for a more snug fit, use the same process to remove the pins that hold the individual links in place. However, if the strap is leather, none of the above applies and you'll need to seek professional assistance.

How To... Fix a Scratched Watch Face

If your watch face picks up scratches and nicks, the fix is simple. Apply a dash of liquid brass polish (plain toothpaste will work just as well) and work over the face with a soft cloth, then clean with a soft damp cloth. Alternatively, stretch clear, non-yellowing art tape (available online) over the face, smoothing down and leaving for twenty-four hours. When you peel off the tape, the adhesive will have filled the scratches.

This entry applies to small scratches, not dirty great cracks. If the face is cracked, seek professional help.

How to... Fix Scratched Sunglasses

General wear and tear can often leave small scratches on your sunglasses, ruining your pretense at effortless cool—here's how to restore your credibility:

FOR GLASS LENSES

Blot a small dollop of white toothpaste onto a cotton wool ball, then onto the scratch, rubbing in small circles to work it into the scratch. Rub for ten to fifteen seconds, then wipe off the toothpaste with a soft, clean cloth, then wipe a damp, soft cloth over it and leave to dry. Repeat until the scratch is as good as invisible.

FOR PLASTIC LENSES

Rinse the scratched lens with warm, soapy water and dry gently with a soft microfiber cloth—paper towels, toilet paper, or anything similarly abrasive may cause more scratches. Dig out a can of furniture polish and spray onto the lens and rub in with a circular motion. This will fill the scratch or scratches with a clear waxy film. Wipe away the excess with a clean, ultra-soft cloth, then repeat on the other side of the lens.

EVERYDAY ELECTRICAL STUFF

By "Everyday Electrical Stuff," we mean televisions and computers, cell phones and digital cameras, and all manner of other fiddly, wire-based business that goes up in a shower of sparks or just turns itself off and dies.

The solutions offered in this section are for simple fixes only; the things that any man or woman can accomplish with their brain still in neutral—no stripping down appliances and tinkering with their wiry innards. Complex jobs should only ever be attempted by a qualified expert who knows what he or she is doing. Not by you. (Unless you're a qualified expert who knows what he's doing. In which case, this book is not for you.)

However, many of the more basic problems can be remedied by the average Joe/Jo, as the following section clearly illustrates.

WARNING!

When attempting to fix any electrical appliance, the first rule is: Take No Chances. If you run the following checks before attempting any of the instructions in this section, you should be safe as houses.

1. Always turn off your home's power supply before you begin, or risk electrocuting yourself to death. That can hurt.

2. Always check your owner's manual before tinkering with anything complicated. If you've lost the manual, check the manufacturer's website for guidelines before you start unscrewing things.

3. Many problems can be remedied by checking that the thing itself is plugged in properly and that the controller has working batteries. Obvious, yes, but these things so often are.

4. Be aware that you risk ruining your warranty by unscrewing the top and poking around its technical bits. If in any doubt at all, have a nice cup of tea and call in a professional.

How to... Fix a Television

The TV's on the blink again, which means that unless you pull your finger out and fix it you'll miss that high-brow documentary on purple-nosed Latvian dung beetles or that reality TV guff you like. Luckily, the problem is often very simple and can be remedied by asking yourself the following questions:

1. Have I consulted the owner's manual that came with the TV, and checked its very handy troubleshooting guide at the back? **YES ☐ NO ☐**

2. Have I seen the manual in recent years? **YES ☐ NO ☐**

If no, does the manufacturer have a useful website that may provide information and advice in an idiot-proof FAQ section? **YES ☐ NO ☐**

3. If that website turns out to be no use, have I tried ringing the manufacturer's help line?
YES, AND IT WAS BLOODY USELESS ☐ NO ☐

4. Have I followed the set-up instructions closely in the manual, aware that failing to set up correctly can result in no sound or no picture, or both? This means making sure that all the connections—AC, freeview, input and output cables—are plugged in correctly. Have I done that? **YES, BUT IT DIDN'T FIX IT ☐ ERM, NO ☐**

5. Did I check to see if the fuse in the circuit box has blown and tripped the switch, flipping it back to "On" if this is the case? **YES ☐ OF COURSE NOT ☐**

6. Do I now regret buying this bargainous 73" Shitachi plasma screen TV from that shifty-looking man in a bar parking lot? **YES, BUT IT WAS ONLY $200! ☐ NO ☐**

7. Might it help if I just pry off the back of the TV with a butter knife, then give these wires a bit of a poke and hope for the best?
YES ☐ ER, NO, I'LL PROBABLY ELECTROCUTE MYSELF TO DEATH ☐

8. Have I kept all the individual parts (vents and speakers, see opposite page) that can be easily cleaned, making sure dust and debris haven't interfered with them and messed things up? Waggled the antenna? Called my friend to see what he thinks as a last resort?
SERIOUSLY, I'VE TRIED EVERYTHING ☐ I'M AT MY WITS' END ☐

9. Have the batteries just gone on the remote?
YES ☐ NO ☐

10. Should I have checked that at the start instead of wasting everybody's time like this?
ERM, BUGGER. SORRY ☐

TV TIPS

Televisions are like cars and nice flowers, in as much as they all demand regular care and attention; otherwise, they'll encounter problems and eventually die on you. To avoid problems down the line, keep dust and debris away from the TV's vents and speakers, because once these get inside and build up, your troubles will begin. Remove dust with a soft cloth regularly to avoid any such buildup.

Moisture around the TV and its complicated electronic bits will also cause problems, so make sure the television is not exposed to excessive moisture and keep a few small packages of silica around the back of the set to absorb any excess.

Finally, to clean the screen and improve your visual experience, use a soft, damp, clean cloth with a mild soap. Never use paper towels or you risk scratching the screen, and never use heavy cleaning products or you risk stripping away your TV's finish over time.

How to... Fix a Remote Control

In an exhaustive study done some time back by a man with too much time on his hands, it was found that the most common fault with TV/DVD/VCR remote controls is caused by a faulty keypad and/or a buildup of greasy deposits on and around the circuit board. Each individual keypad should push down smoothly and make clean contact with the internal circuit board, making it painless to switch from *American Idol* to *Law & Order*, or whatever it is you gawk at. Over time though, grease and gunk will cake up the pads, meaning you have to push with greater force every time you want to change channel. The following will help you fix it:

Step 1. Remove the batteries, placing them safely to one side.

Step 2. Unscrew the screws on your control and keep them safe too, then take a blunt knife and carefully pry the remote apart by sliding the knife into the join and pushing gently upward to open it up. You should now have two parts (ignoring the plastic cover)—one is the key panel, the other the circuit board.

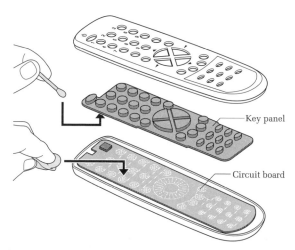

Key panel

Circuit board

Step 3. Remove any dirt or grease from the circuit board by gently wiping with a damp cloth and mild detergent or rubbing alcohol. The circuit board can be very easily damaged, so wipe slowly and very lightly and use the liquid sparingly. Leave it to dry, noting the grotty black stain on your cloth, before wiping once more with another clean cloth.

Step 4. Using a cotton ball dipped in your detergent or alcohol, gently clean the contacts on the remote's keyboard that make the connection to the circuit board.

Step 5. Dry thoroughly, then piece the remote back together by reversing the first two steps, and you are now free to channel surf once more to your heart's content.

How to... Troubleshoot a Digital Camera

Point and click. Point and click. Point and click. It couldn't be easier until, one day, you point and click but there is no click. Then you're annoyed. If you're lucky, you may be able to fix the problem yourself, using one of the very simple suggestions detailed below.

PROBLEM 1. THE CAMERA DOESN'T TURN ON

Check 1. If the camera takes batteries, check that they have power (and if they are rechargeable, check that they have been charged).

Check 2. Make sure the batteries have been correctly inserted too, with plus touching plus and minus touching minus.

Check 3. If you have an AC adapter, connect it to the camera and attempt to turn it on. If it now turns on, this suggests that the batteries need changing.

Check 4. If all of the above fails, ask yourself if the memory card is full. If it is, the camera may not turn on. Remove the batteries for twenty-four hours and try again. If it turns on now, you'll need to make space on the memory card by deleting things you don't need.

And if this doesn't work, the camera is a goner, as they say in the trade. As a last resort, consult the troubleshooting guide you received when you bought it, but it is most likely that you'll need to have it fixed by an expert.

PROBLEM 2. THE SCREEN KEEPS TURNING OFF

Check 1. The screen should give you a strong hint as to why it's turning off before it dies on you—words or an icon will appear on screen and give you a warning. Usually, it'll be a low battery that needs charging, or the camera's simply set on "power-save" mode, which will make it close down after a predetermined period of time. Consult the camera manual for details on how to change the setting, via the menu.

Check 2. The camera may also close down if the battery is too cold. Remove the battery, nurse it back to room temperature, and try again.

PROBLEM 3. THE CAMERA WON'T LET ME TAKE PICTURES

Check 1. If the memory is full, the camera won't take any more shots. Check if this is the case and delete any shabby shots or copy them to a computer.

Check 2. Make sure that the camera has not been switched to review mode, where you will only be able to see images that you have taken, and not take fresh images.

Check 3. As ever, make sure the batteries are in full working condition. If the power light remains on but the camera seems to be frozen, locate the reset button and press it.

PROBLEM 4. THE FLASH WON'T WORK

Check 1. Once again, it'll be something very simple, such as spent batteries or you've inadvertently knocked the settings onto no-flash mode. Check and amend if so.

Check 2. Also, don't be so hasty to push down the button you use to take a snap—you need to give the flash time to fully charge before taking a shot.

How To... Fix a Faulty Cell Phone

Too many fiddly little faults can plague your precious cell phone for us to cover in any real depth here, so let's concentrate on some basic troubleshooting that should stand you in good stead if, or when, the phone inexplicably stops working.

PROBLEM 1. THE POWER CYCLE

Otherwise known as turning the phone off and back on again. A simple fix, no question, but this often cures a whole host of ailments, including lack of signal and faulty keys. Because your phone is on duty for so long day in, day out, often all it needs is a little breather.

PROBLEM 2. YOU NEED TO RESET

Like the power cycle, only bigger and better. Every cell phone should have a factory reset button, hidden away inside the settings. Press this and although you'll lose your snazzy ring tone and screen saver, your phone may well return from the dead.

PROBLEM 3. THE BATTERY

If the phone turns off unexpectedly or you find you're having to charge it for progressively longer periods between uses, the battery may be drained and need replacing. Before you buy a replacement, though, check that the SIM card is correctly inserted and that it's free of dust and grime. A loose SIM can also cause a cell phone to close down unexpectedly. Clean the contacts on both the battery and the SIM with a soft, clean cloth, re-insert, and test again. If the problem persists, buy a new battery.

PROBLEM 4. WATER DAMAGE

More complicated, this. You'll need to act fast if water gets inside your cell phone—electricity and water obviously don't mix. The key is to dry the phone's internals very quickly and let the phone dry out. To do this, do this:

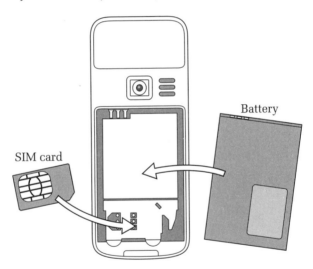

Battery

SIM card

Step 1. Remove the battery and SIM card and pat dry.

Step 2. Gently shake the phone to remove as much of the water as possible, as quickly as possible, then use a soft cloth to get into all gaps and slots.

Step 3. Vacuum the handset dry with a soft brush—your aim is to pull any vapor out, rather than push it farther in (so never use a hair dryer for this).

Step 4. When you've dried the phone as much as possible, leave it sitting in a bowl of silica gel overnight. This will draw out the last drops of water you can't reach.

Step 5. Check the next day and if it's still moist, vacuum again and leave to sit for another twenty-four hours.

Step 6. When the phone is bone-dry, piece back together and turn on. If it doesn't turn on, plug it into its charger without the battery and test. If now it does turn on, the battery is damaged and needs to be replaced. If that still doesn't work, seek expert help.

PROBLEM 5. NONE OF THE ABOVE

The phone still won't work? You, plucky amateur, have done as much as you can. Call your phone company or return the phone to the shop it was bought from and angrily demand your money back. Well, it's got to be worth a try.

How To... Troubleshoot a Faulty Telephone

Landline phones generally go wrong in one of two ways: Either you cannot receive calls or you cannot make them. Either way, your line to the outside world (i.e., the police and pizza delivery man) is severed, and that's no good. Luckily, there are several simple tests you can run on a faulty phone line.

PROBLEM 1. YOU CAN'T RECEIVE CALLS

Nobody has called in ages, which either suggests that nobody likes you or that the phone has run into some kind of problem. Let's go with the latter option and run through some very basic tests you can do.

Test 1. Make sure that the telephone is plugged in correctly and that the ringer hasn't somehow been switched off or set on a low ring that you can't hear.

Test 2. Check the REN value—every phone has a Ringing Equivalent Number, usually of 1, that should be noted on its base. There's a limited amount of power available from your phone company to make your phones ring. Exceed that limit—which is usually four or five when adding the REN value of all connected equipment together—and your phone will stop ringing. Your problem may be remedied by taking one or more items (an answering machine, fax, etc.) out of the phone line to reduce the REN value.

Test 3. Make sure the phone sits on a hard surface. Many house phones have the bell built into the base of the telephone—a soft surface can nullify the ring tone.

PROBLEM 2. YOU CAN'T MAKE CALLS

You dial the number but the call never gets through. You'll obviously have the right area code for the call you're trying to make. Obviously. And if the problem persists, you'll also have called another number in a different area or part of the country to make sure it's not just a service problem affecting that one number. Those things are obviously obvious but often overlooked.

A more advanced solution is to unplug all equipment (answering machine, fax, etc.) on the phone line and plug the phone directly into the main telephone socket with nothing else attached. This will show you if the fault is with the phone or with your cables. If the phone works, replace the line. If the phone still doesn't work, in this instance you'll have to replace it with a nice new one.

How to... Clean a Scratched Disc (CD or DVD)

If your CD or DVD disc jumps or freezes mid-play, it's either stained or scratched. The former is far easier to fix than the latter, but they're both salvageable. Let's start with the easy one.

OPTION 1. REMOVING STAINS AND IMPERFECTIONS

To remove fingerprints, dust, and grease, run the disc under warm water. Avoid strong cleaners, abrasives, or acids, which may damage the disc's delicate data. Icy cold water can stress the disc, so make certain you only ever use lukewarm water on it.

If the stain's stubborn, rub very gently with a clean finger (your finger, ideally) and only ever rub from the center out to the edge to prevent further scratching: Rub round in a circular pattern and you risk causing more damage to the data stored on the disc.

Shake off excess water and let the disc dry naturally, away from bright light that can cause yet more damage, then try in the player again.

OPTION 2. REMOVING SCRATCHES

The worst scratches run in the same direction as the spiral on the disc—those dirty great scratches that run from the center to the edge of the disc look far worse but are often less damaging and often don't need to be addressed.

If you're struggling to isolate the offending scratch, play the disc and note which section is most affected (this is more easily done with a CD than a DVD)—the disc tracks start from the center and play outward, making it slightly easier to judge.

Once you've isolated the scratch, you'll need to gently buff at it with a safe solution:

Step 1. Place the upturned disc on a surface that is flat and stable but *not abrasive* (the label side is close to the disc's data and can be damaged far more easily than the bottom side so must not be placed on a rough surface). If you bugger the top of the disc, it may never work again. If the top appears to be damaged, be warned that the following advice, while still worth trying, may not save your disc.

Step 2. Take a clean, lint-free cloth and apply a small dab of either plain white toothpaste with baking soda or Brasso, then very gently rub the cloth along the scratch from the disc's inner circle to outer edge, rather than in a circular motion that can cause yet more damage.

Step 3. Repeat this process several times.

Step 4. Remove the toothpaste with warm water and allow it to dry before wiping once more with a clean white cloth. If you used Brasso, simply wipe it clean with a cloth.

Step 5. To avoid damaging your DVD or CD player, all discs should be completely free of moisture when you insert them. Once you're happy the disc is clean and dry, try it again in your player.

Step 6. If it still jumps, make sure you buffed up the correct scratch. If you did but the problem persists, the scratch may be too deep to repair. This disc should probably therefore be thrown away and put down to experience. Before doing so, however, read the next section in case the problem lies with your CD/DVD player and not the disc after all.

How to... Clean a CD or DVD Player

If you've checked that the disc itself is clean and unscratched (see page 50) but it still sticks or jumps when you play it, your only other hope is to clean the laser pick-up within the player. The pick-up looks like an eye and reads the information on the disc—and it needs to be whistle-clean to function properly. Luckily, fixing it isn't especially demanding.

Step 1. Insert a lens cleaner disc. These cost very little and can rectify the problem without you having to resort to poking around inside the machine. Only if this doesn't solve the problem should you proceed to Step 2.

Step 2. Remove the CD and unplug the player—to avoid electric shocks and all that. Unscrew the player's top and keep the screws safe because you'll need them again very soon.

Step 3. With the top off, you can now access the laser and the rails it slides along. The player reads the information on the disc by running its laser beam out of its eye and along the tracking, sweeping across its spiral track from the center to the outside edge of the disc. If the laser isn't sweeping along its track precisely, your disc won't play properly, no matter how much you raise your voice at it. Cleaning these rails may provide the answer, so take a small gloop of WD-40 on your cotton ball and carefully grease the rails.

Tracks Laser   Rail

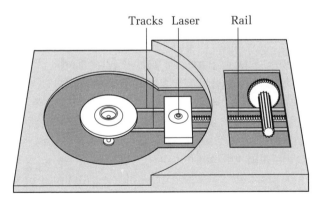

Step 4. Next, locate the large (and therefore unmissable) cog-type wheel inside the machine and gently turn it

by hand. This will move the laser along the track, allowing you to grease the section of rail beneath the laser that had previously been out of sight.

Step 5. Take another cotton ball and dip it in ethanol, squeeze it to leave it damp but not dripping, then gently run this over the lens of the laser.

Step 6. When the ethanol has dried, screw the whole thing back together and turn the player back on. If it has worked, insert a CD/DVD and indulge in a celebratory dance of delight.

Step 7. Or, if it's a jazz disc, just sit there gently stroking your funny little beard.

How to... Fix a Faulty Vinyl Record

Not strictly an electrical, this, but it's at home beside the CD fixes for any retro readers who haven't yet upgraded. Now records are generally made of vinyl, which, being thin and delicate, can mess up very easily and in a number of ways. Three of the most common are detailed as follows:

TO FIX A SCRATCHED RECORD

Step 1. The easiest approach is to observe where the record is scratched; watch and listen until the music skips. When it does, look at the record and you will have located the scratch.

Step 2. Lift the needle from the record and turn the player off. Then place the needle back on the record, as close to the scratched section as possible, and play it backward, rotating the record manually.

Step 3. As the needle goes across the grooves it should smooth out any scratches, but you will need to go over the record a number of times for it to succeed. Work gently and slowly to avoid causing greater damage, and if this doesn't correct things, you'll need expert assistance.

TO STRAIGHTEN A WARPED RECORD

So easy this one—just place the record between two sheets of glass and leave it to sit in the sun for a while. We're not talking a swelteringly hot sun that melts things, but a pleasant heat that will gently heat and straighten the vinyl.

TO CLEAN A FILTHY RECORD

Vinyl is delicate, and anything caustic may melt your precious long-player, but a simple solution of detergent and water will remove any grimy grot that can stick in the grooves and mess up your music. Hold the record by the edges, so you do not touch the grooves, then dip it into the solution, making sure the papery middle section doesn't get wet. Rotate the record, then rinse it in tepid water and gently wipe dry with a soft cloth. It should play like new again now.

How to... Troubleshoot a Video Player

If, unlike the rest of the world, you haven't upgraded to DVD, or Blu-ray, or whatever has inevitably come along since you began reading this paragraph, then this is how to remedy some of the more common VCR problems you will eventually encounter.

PROBLEM 1. FLICKERING PICTURE

If the player is acting up and you have a flickering picture, check to see if the tape is faulty by ejecting and replacing with another. It might be the tape, not the player, which would save you all the head scratching. If it *is* the tape, go to Problem 4.

If changing the tape makes no difference, your other option is to tweak the tracking. All VCRs should have a tracking knob, which will normally be on the front panel of your VCR, though it's sometimes round the back. Find it, play the tape, and turn the knob either left or right until the picture improves enough to watch. Just the ticket.

PROBLEM 2. NO SOUND AND/OR PICTURE

Unplug the VCR and check all the other connections are plugged in correctly—VCR to TV, the AC plug into the wall, and output cables. Make sure the VCR is on the TV setting. And while you are there, unplug and wipe the video with a soft, clean cloth for good measure, taking the opportunity to clean any other parts that can be cleaned without you digging around and risking more damage—we're talking knobs and buttons here. If this fails, a last-resort option is to turn off the video, unplug it, and leave it for a few minutes—a power surge can often confuse the VCR's simple-minded microcomputer, but turning off and unplugging the machine can often reset it. After a few minutes, turn it back on and try again. If this fails, it almost certainly needs a professional fix.

PROBLEM 3. THE PICTURE/SOUND IS THERE BUT IT'S JIGGERED

If the sound is intermittent or the picture distorted, or both, adjusting the tracking can resolve the problem. Once you've found the tracking knob (see Problem 1), tweak left or right until the picture/sound returns to normal, but return the knob to the neutral position when you've finished watching whatever you've been watching.

PROBLEM 4. THE PICTURE IS SNOWY

You'll almost certainly need to clean the tape heads, because over time old video tapes can leave a terrible oxide deposit on your VCR's tape heads. In turn, this can create the snowy picture you're now experiencing, which is fine during *Ski Sunday* but a world of pain during *Rambo: First Blood*.

The solution—or at least *a* solution—is to let a new blank tape play in the VCR for an hour. This will often clean the heads and remedy the situation without you needing to trouble yourself.

Failing that, a head-cleaning tape you can buy online will effortlessly clean the heads while you sit back and drink tea. Buy one that uses cleaning fluid, rather than the dry-cleaning alternative, because the solution used in a fluid cleaner is more effective for removing tape-head gunk. Try this also if your VCR plays videos but won't record.

PROBLEM 5. TAPE JAM*

If the VCR refuses to release the tape, turn the video player off, unplug it, and leave it for a few minutes. As before, if the VCR has become befuddled, turning it on and off can often be enough to correct things. However, if it's not, your only hope may be to delve inside the machine. This is risky as fiddling with the insides could well ruin any warranty you have, but if you're prepared to risk it, switch the power off at

---

*This procedure assumes there are no broken parts or foreign objects or other damage that will stop you turning the mechanism. If there are, seek professional help.

the mains, unscrew the top of your recorder, keeping the screws safe and noting where each one lived. Once inside, don't just yank at the tape and do not try to force it—you're guaranteed to inflict more damage.

Instead, if your VCR is like most VCRs, you'll see a large gear wheel near the front of the tape. Carefully unloop the tape from the VCR head, then turn that wheel by hand and it should release the tape and allow you to remove it from the machine. A tape jam often indicates the tape itself is damaged, rather than the machine. Discard if it's broken, then replace the VCR cover and put it down to experience.

How to... Troubleshoot a Computer

It won't turn on. It's a common problem. So, imagine the following questions being fired at you by a patronizing and uninterested I.T. operative on the other end of a customer service line.

1. Yeah, computer's dead? You turned it on?
YES ☐ **NO** ☐

2. Is that big power cable round the back plugged in properly? Yeah, both ends, one into the back of the computer, the other into a power source. Yeah, by power source I obviously mean a plug socket but am trying to complicate matters. **YES** ☐ **NO** ☐

3. But is that power source even working? Try another electrical item in the socket to check that it's fully functional. **YES** ☐ **NO** ☐

4. Have you checked that all the cables—keyboard, monitor, and mouse—are plugged in properly?
YES ☐ **NO** ☐
If yes, check them again, but unplug them all and re-plug securely again. And check the fuse in the plug while you're at it and replace it if necessary.

5. Does your computer have a surge protector with a reset button? **YES** ☐ **NO** ☐

How to... Boost FM Radio Reception

A radio signal suffers the farther away from the transmitter you are, and when large buildings and rolling hills block the signal's path to your house. The ideal solution would be to move much closer to the transmitter, thereby guaranteeing the clearest, crispest reception imaginable with none of the hissing interference. However, that being a totally impractical suggestion, you might like to consider the following instead:

Option 1. Move the radio towards an open area—toward a window would certainly be a start—to minimize the risk of interference. Once you've done that, extend the radio's telescopic aerial and point it towards the transmitter. Unless you live in the shadow of your closest transmitter (in which case your reception should be A1 anyway), this will require a little research on your part—check one of the various online resources detailing where your local transmitters are positioned and point the aerial that-a-way.

Option 2. Flicking the switch from "stereo" to "mono" can help, as can pressing the AFC switch on radios that have them. Look for the letters "A," "F," and "C," in that order, and press to reduce distortion.

Option 3. Connect an external antenna or a TV antenna to your radio for a signal boost, if you have the option.

Look on the back of the unit for a screw or plug-type connection marked with the letters ANT or FM ANT and ask someone in your local electrical shop which antenna works best for your radio.

How to... Make a Vacuum Cleaner Suck Up More*

A vacuum cleaner that stops picking up dust and debris is no good to you—before you know it you'll be knee-deep in dead skin and other festering grime. Luckily, you can remedy the situation with a few basic tweaks here and there.

Filter bag

Filters

Hose

Brush

*This fix applies to both upright and canister cleaners.

Check 1. Inspect the hose (see diagram) for blockages as hair and debris can easily build up and reduce airflow, but they can just as easily be removed by hand or by poking an unfurled coat hanger through the hole and "waggling it about a bit," as they probably say in the trade.

Unscrew and examine the ends of the tubing for blockages; drop a coin through the hose to test; if it comes out cleanly, you almost certainly don't have a blockage. If it doesn't, you almost certainly do. Clear any remaining blockages and pocket the coin before turning on the vacuum again; otherwise, it could rattle around inside and cause damage.

Finally, check to see that the vacuum's hose is in full working order. If it has any cracks along its length, covering them up tightly with duct tape will increase suction.

Check 2. If the vacuum has a filter bag, check for blockages in the opening; these too can significantly reduce a vacuum's suction. Also, if the bag is moist or damp after vacuuming wet areas, its sucking power will again be reduced. Replace the bag—as you should aim to do every six months or so anyway—and avoid hoovering over damp patches in future.

Check 3. Make sure the filters are not clogged up by dirt and debris. If they're removable, wash the filters by hand with a mild soap and warm water, and replace with new filters at least once a year to guarantee you get maximum suction.

Check 4. Finally, check the vacuum's brush for more hair blockages. If these occur, the air will not flow correctly. Pull out any blockages by hand and discard, or weave into a small toupee for a mouse.

WHITE GOODS (BIG AND SMALL)

The white goods we refer to here are the washing machines, refrigerators, and dishwashers that will suddenly start to shake, rattle, and roll across the floor for no obvious reason, then spring a leak, leaving you standing in a puddle of sudsy water scratching your head. They are also the blender that will no longer blend, the toaster that won't toast, and the kettle that boils up water that tastes like raw sewage. White goods come in all shapes and sizes and can break down on you in any number of ways. Luckily, most of them can be fixed without much fuss or drama.

WARNING!

The fixes that follow are all included because they are straightforward and safe for the average layman/woman to perform. If you find yourself considering tinkering with wires or stripping things down... DON'T. These jobs should *always* be left to an expert.

Also, with any fix involving water, make damn sure you turn off the water supply to the appliance you are fixing first, or risk being soaked or saturating your floor and making the problem ten times worse.

How to... Fix a Kettle

The most common kettle complaint is not that it won't actually work, but that it has started to boil up water that tastes like it was dredged from the drains. This is caused by limescale, a hard, chalky deposit found in hard water areas that builds up over time inside the kettle. You could move to another part of the country where the water's softer, or you could throw the kettle away and buy a new one, but both options are extreme and against the spirit of this tome. So, instead, the solution is to de-scale the kettle, which is very easily done following two simple steps:

Step 1. Fill the kettle with a 50/50 mix of cold water and white vinegar and boil it up. You'll need to leave this fetid brew to sit for twenty-four hours, which means you'll either need to boil your water in a pan on the stove like they did in The War, or consume only cold beverages for a while.

Step 2. After twenty-four hours have passed, scrub at the kettle's innards with an old toothbrush to dislodge any stubborn limescale, then replace it with fresh water and boil it again. Rinse with this water and the de-scaling is complete—your kettle should be as good as new. And if there's still a faint taste of vinegar, boil and rinse one more time.

AN ALTERNATIVE SOLUTION

Some people—impatient types and those with a more maverick streak—suggest pouring a can of cola into your kettle and leaving overnight to clean its innards and rid the kettle of all limescale. Rinse thoroughly afterward, obviously, otherwise your hot beverage will taste of sugary gloop that rots your teeth.

How to... Mend a Malfunctioning Microwave Oven

The microwave oven is the single most dangerous thing you'll find in your kitchen, unless you invite a serial killer round for tea. Even then it would run him close because of the fearsomely high voltages and currents that lurk within the microwave's casing. And when you unplug the oven from the wall, it lives on thanks to a high voltage capacitor that retains a dangerous charge and keeps it armed and unsafe for some time. Exposing the cover and poking around inside with a screwdriver is asking for trouble and could leave you dead (with a mop of frizzy, singed hair). So, if your microwave breaks down on you and requires anything other than the most basic trouble-shooting (as detailed in the next few pages), contact a trained professional and let him risk his life. However, for simple solutions, consider the following:

PROBLEM 1. THE MICROWAVE HAS STOPPED WORKING

Step 1. If the microwave is switched on at the plug and all the connections appear to be OK, check the fuse. Often, the microwave's fuse can blow if the door is slammed too hard, and a blown fuse will stop the microwave working.

Step 2. The fuse usually lives inside the microwave casing, so unscrew the retaining screws and carefully remove the cabinet (i.e., the outer casing).

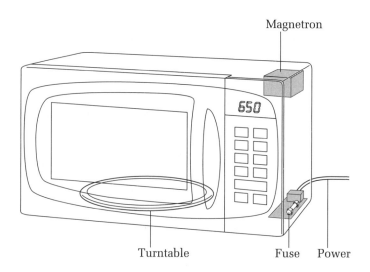

Magnetron

650

Turntable   Fuse   Power

Step 3. Follow the power cord into the unit and it'll lead to the fuse holder—the fuse itself is cylindrical, about an inch or so long and with metallic ends. If it's blown, it will look blackened and burnt.

Step 4. Even if it doesn't appear to have blown, replace it while you're there, just to be on the safe side. However, make sure it's of the **exact same type and rating**; otherwise, it may blow again and cause greater problems.

Step 5. Replace the cabinet, plug the microwave back in, and test to see if it works properly again. Oh, and a general, but vital, rule to mention here is that you should never run the microwave with nothing inside. It ruins the magnetron (which essentially powers your microwave) and compounds your problems.

PROBLEM 2. THERE ARE SPARKS INSIDE THE MICROWAVE

This is most likely to be caused by something in the oven that disagrees with the microwaves bouncing around, so...

Step 1. Look for any aluminum items and anything with a metallic edge or trim; these are scientifically proven to cause sparks and play hell with microwave ovens.

Step 2. Keep an eye out also for any chipped or peeling microwave paint—if this has left an exposed metal surface, you'll have the same problem, so repaint with a suitable heat-resistant paint or epoxy.

Step 3. Also, you can expect sparks—or what the professionals call "electrical arcing"—if you've left food or burned remnants in the cooking chamber. Clean thoroughly, sanding away burn spots if soap and water won't suffice. Touch up with a suitable paint if required.

PROBLEM 3. THE TURNTABLE WON'T TURN

A non-turning turntable is merely a table, which is no good when it comes to microwaving food.

Step 1. See if the rollers and tracks the turntable runs on are properly aligned, or if debris is blocking the turntable, preventing it from turning cleanly.

Step 2. Make sure the glass tray on which you place receptacles is also fitted correctly and turning smoothly.

Step 3. Remove the tray from the microwave and wash thoroughly to remove any debris that may be causing trouble. Any parts that can be removed and cleaned should be, making sure they are pieced back together as the man who made the microwave intended.

Step 4. When you insert any big pots into the microwave, make sure they are not so large that they bang and clank against the walls, as this will prevent a safe and smooth rotation of the turntable.

If the turning mechanism looks to have broken, however, it will need taking apart and replacing—and this, unfortunately, is a job for a fully qualified expert.

PROBLEM 4. THE MICROWAVE WON'T HEAT UP

Step 1. For a microwave to work properly, and provide the required heat, its walls need to be free of built-up gunk and crusty dried-on crap; otherwise, the waves won't bounce cleanly around the interior and heat up your food. Get into the habit of wiping all walls clean with a mild detergent, warm water, and a clean sponge after every use.

Step 2. Listen also for any unusual sounds, particularly a suspicious buzzing noise that could well point to problems within the magnetron—your microwave's main generator. If it buzzes, it could well be broken and will need replacing by a qualified professional.

PROBLEM 5. THE CONTROL TOUCH PADS HAVE STOPPED WORKING

The best case scenario here is that they're just wet after cleaning, which you need to do every so often or risk a buildup of grime and, oddly, small insects drawn in by the stench of food and the warmth of the circuit board. Once the pads have thoroughly dried out, they should be fine again. Keeping each individual button free from any grime and insects is advisable, but avoid using excess water or the pads may give up the ghost completely.

How to... Sharpen Blender Blades

Blunt blades on a blender are no use when you need to turn bulky vegetables into mush in the blink of an eye. You need them to be dangerously sharp and whirring at a truly terrifying rate of knots. If they're not, the following four-step action plan should help:

Step 1. For safety's sake, turn the blender off before you begin—even if the blades are blunt, they could still lop your fingers off. Blenders get sluggish over time, but usually it's nothing more than residue obstructing the blade, which can be removed by hand. So lift the blades out and gently wipe or brush them clean.

Step 2. If the residue is more stubborn, fill the blender with one cup of baking soda and an equal measure of water. Leave it to stand and eat into the gunk for an hour or two, then turn the machine on and really blitz the buildup. Rinse with hot water for a textbook finish.

Step 3. To reinvigorate dull blades, fill the blender halfway with warm, soapy water and run on high for ten seconds before adding a few cubes of ice to the mixture and running again. Repeat if required and this will miraculously sharpen the blades, extend your blender's life, and save you the bother of going out and buying a new one.

Step 4. Finally, if the blades appear sharp enough but they judder and wobble as they rotate, you may need to adjust the drive stud; this isn't difficult. Just remove the blender's base and look for the drive shaft—the bottom of it should protrude from the bottom of the motor—and on that you'll find the drive stud, holding the whole thing in place. It needs to be tight to secure the blades, so tighten with pliers if loose, taking care not to overtighten it. If it looks to be worn or damaged in any way, unscrew and replace it with a new stud of the exact same dimensions.

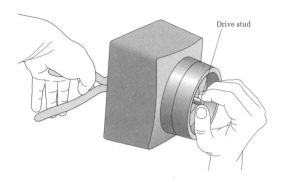

Drive stud

How to... Troubleshoot Your Toaster

Toasters are designed to carry the bread down into the fiery pits on a carriage, but as that carriage goes down and then jolts back up, it inevitably sends loose bread crumbs down into the bottom of the toaster where, over time, they build up and clog the mechanism. These must be removed for the mechanism to operate smoothly, so follow these easy steps to get your toast popping up properly again:

Step 1. Unplug the toaster and carry it to the trash can.

Step 2. If the toaster has been designed with a removable crumb tray, remove said tray and tip the crumbs into the trash can.

Step 3. Gently tap both sides of the toaster and turn it upside down to dislodge any other crumbs stuck in the machine. Don't shake vigorously or you may dislodge or damage its sensitive heating elements and the toaster itself will be toast. If you're feeling particularly thorough, use a can of compressed air or a small clean brush to dislodge any really stubborn buildup.

Step 4. This is where a more complex Step 4 solution should be, only there isn't one. Eradicating crumbs is the key to maintaining a healthy, happy toaster. Leave them in there to fester and a simple carriage blockage can lead on to more serious problems—the crumbs can damage the heating element, interfere with the solenoid operation (which releases the latch), and plug the latch release, making it impossible to get a decent slice of toast in the morning. To head off such issues, make a mental note to clean your toaster at least once a week.

WARNING!

If those basic crumb removal tips don't work, the toaster's problem may be more complicated and involve a faulty element, solenoid, or thermostat. In most cases, this would require you to take the toaster apart and fiddle with its internal organs, which would be dangerous. At best, you could end up with loads of small nuts and bolts scattered about the table, and at worst, several thousand volts coursing through your body. Seek expert help.

How to... Fix a Leaking Washing Machine

Water inside the machine is a good thing, an absolute necessity even. A great puddle of sudsy water spilling out across your kitchen floor is less good and will need to be fixed right away. Luckily, it's a common ailment, and diagnosing the source of the leak is often the biggest problem.

WARNING!

Before running through the checks below, and to avoid a good soaking, make sure your washing machine is switched off at the mains and that you have turned off the water supply.

CHECK 1. LOOSE PIPE CONNECTIONS

They'll be around the back of the machine and should all be tightened if they've come even slightly loose.

CHECK 2. WEAR AND TEAR

Damage around the door seal—the rubber seal that bridges the drum with the outer case and runs around the door—can cause chaos. Ordinarily, the seal stops water leaking out, but it can split through general wear and tear and will need replacing if this is the problem, by an expert. Not you. With respect.

CHECK 3. THE DRAIN PIPE

This carries the waste water out to the main drain via a U-shaped bend (see below), but it can easily become clogged up with a soapy blockage that sends the water shooting back from whence it came and spills out onto your kitchen floor. Follow the drain pipe out from the back of the machine, locate the U-bend, and carefully dismantle it. Remove the blockage by hand and reattach the U-bend.

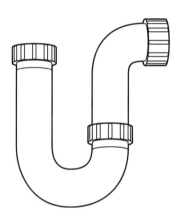

CHECK 4. THE SOAP DRAWER

This can often spill over because of blockages caused by overfilling with washing powder. If the powder is not being dissolved each time you wash, a soapy gunk will eventually build up and cause water to again spill out. You can remedy this by removing any excess soap by hand, then washing the remainder away by slooshing boiling water into the soap drawer. Repeat if necessary, and repeat again until the blockage has been removed.

If none of the above apply and the leak continues, the machine may be overfilling and spilling out onto your floor due to a faulty water level sensor. This will need replacing but is a complex, fiddly procedure best left to a plumber.

How to... Kickstart an Underperforming Washing Machine

A hefty slug of white vinegar is the answer here. A buildup of limescale in your washing machine's drum and internal pipes can hamper its performance and make you think about slinging it out and buying a new one. That would be wasteful, particularly as you can often fix the problem by simply pouring a dash of white vinegar into the powder drawer and running the washer as normal, on your usual cycle. This magical medicinal brew will cut through limescale and boost performance levels in double-quick time.

How To... Fix a Noisy Washing Machine

All washing machines are noisy, but your ears shouldn't bleed when you stand in range of it. It seems you have one of two problems.

Problem 1. The most likely cause is that you've just overloaded the machine with clothes, causing the drum to overbalance and clunk and clank during the spin cycle. If so, stop the washer and remove some of the clothes and start again.

Problem 2. If the machine is one of those that shakes and shudders and dances about the room, the most likely cause is that its four feet are no longer at the same level—the result of months or years of juddering about with a full load in its belly. Place a spirit level across the top of the washer between the back two feet, take a reading, and use an adjustable wrench to bring them back into line. Repeat on the remaining three sides of the machine, but bear in mind that shorter feet will give you more stability.

If this doesn't cure your problem, however, then your floor is possibly uneven and you might want to consider moving house. Or it's a more complicated problem, and you know who you'll have to call...

How to... Fix a Washing Machine Door That Won't Open

Balls. This is bad. All your underwear is inside and you have no fresh pairs for the week ahead and you'll have to go commando. Oh no!

Panic not. If you've established that you've not been fooled by a time-delay mechanism and that the machine isn't just waiting for the water to drain away before it opens (which usually takes a minute at the end of the wash cycle), you'll need to investigate the machine's interlock. Although models vary, the lock can often be reached by removing the top cover. If so, and ensuring the machine is switched off at the mains first, feel around inside for the interlock, which sits behind the hole where the door catch enters the main case and can often be disengaged by hand with a stout tug. If this works but the problem persists, the mechanism will need to be replaced. By an expert. As it will if the interlock is not accessible through the top.

How to... Fix an Underperforming Dishwasher

A common ailment, this, and one which can be caused not so much by mechanical malfunctions as by stupidity: Refer to your owner's manual to make sure that you're loading the dishwasher correctly. Shove all your dirty dishes in half-cocked, with larger items at the front and smaller ones at the back, and you may block the all-important spray arm (the arm that sprays water around the washer). It can't spray effectively if its path is blocked by overhanging handles or poorly stacked plates. However, having said all that, the problem could just as easily be caused by the spray arm being bunged up with gunk—i.e., flakes of limescale or food that get caught in the spray holes. This can be easily remedied:

Step 1. Unplug the dishwasher and turn the power supply off, then remove the spray arm or arms by unclipping or unscrewing the retaining nut.

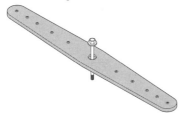

Step 2. Rinse away the gunk and use a toothpick to clean out any blockages before reattaching the arm. This should restore it to full working order.

Also, be aware that cold water will not clean a plate. The water temperature needs to be set at around 120°F (50°C) to effectively dissolve the combination of soap and grease. Finally, it is worth noting that to ensure maximum water pressure and a better performance, make sure that no other water-fueled appliances are running when the dishwasher is switched on.

How To... Fix a Faulty Refrigerator

To keep your sausages cold and your butter from melting, a refrigerator needs to be kept at exactly the right temperature—which it won't be if it's on the blink.

Often, the problem will be one of two things: The temperature controls malfunction or the condenser coils need a good cleaning. Let's take them in order:

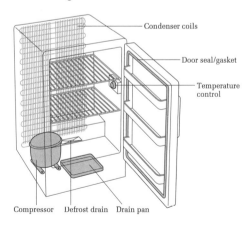

Condenser coils

Door seal/gasket

Temperature control

Compressor   Defrost drain   Drain pan

PROBLEM 1. THE TEMPERATURE CONTROLS MALFUNCTION

First, be aware that a new refrigerator can take twenty-four hours for the temperature to drop to the required level, so if you've only just bought the thing, relax and sleep on it. If the refrigerator's not new and its innards are too warm, check the temperature controls. These are almost always located inside the refrigerator and can be accidentally knocked while you're putting your foodstuffs away. Refer to your manual's temperature guide and adjust as necessary.

The temperature can also be affected by people constantly opening the refrigerator door—particularly in the freezer and the fresh food compartments—so consider a padlock, or set the temperature slightly lower to compensate.

PROBLEM 2. THE CONDENSER COILS

The condenser coils are the mini radiators through which cold air constantly flows around the fridge to keep the temperature down. Over time, these coils can collect dust and debris that can cause them to overheat, hum annoyingly, send your energy bills through the roof, and spoil all your cheese. The coils, therefore, should be serviced twice a year to keep them clean. To see how to do this yourself, turn over the page.

Step 1. Unplug the refrigerator and locate said coils—they're normally rear- or floor-mounted, and usually hidden behind a removable plate.

Step 2. Carefully brush or vacuum away the dust and apply a mild soap and water solution if it's a more stubborn buildup.

Step 3. If your refrigerator has a fan running on the back, locate the access panel and remove any potential buildup or blockages in the same way.

WARNING!

The fridge is a complex character, and no good will ever come from jiggling it about or tipping it upside down. It might make you feel better giving it a good kick, but it won't make your fridge miraculously start working properly. As a general rule you should always keep your refrigerator (and freezer) in the upright position to avoid causing damage that will cost big money to repair. And if you find yourself thinking about tinkering with the wiring at the back, don't. Spending your hard-earned cash is often avoidable, as this book shows you, but if it prevents you electrocuting yourself, do it.

TAKING A TEMPERATURE

To test the temperature in the fridge, remove all food and set the thermostat to its lowest setting. Place a glass of cold tap water in the middle of the fridge for twenty-four hours, then take its temperature with a fridge thermometer. It should read between 32–41ºF. If the temperature doesn't fall between 32–41ºF, check the thermostat sensor hasn't become caked in food, as that would give a false reading. If the sensor is clean, the thermostat is likely to be faulty and will need replacing by a qualified professional.

How to... Fix a Leaking Refrigerator

A small puddle of water at the base of the fridge is mildly alarming but not unusual—nor indeed cause for any great concern. In most cases, it's caused by one of four basic ailments:

PROBLEM 1. YOU HAVE A LEAKING DRAIN PAN

This pan is in place to catch condensation and prevent it spilling out onto your floor, but if it's damaged, it won't do its job. It usually lives underneath the unit and can be accessed by removing the grill at the bottom of the refrigerator (though as always, refer to your user manual if in any doubt). Locate the pan, carefully pull it out, and inspect it, pouring out any accumulated water. Check for leaks and fill with a waterproof sealant or replace the entire pan if necessary (contact the manufacturer of your refrigerator in this instance).

PROBLEM 2. YOU HAVE A FAULTY DEFROST DRAIN

Like the drain pan, the defrost drain also removes condensation and is usually located beneath the vegetable trays or along the floor of the freezer compartment, though models vary and you should consult your manual. Check to make sure this is not clogged or cracked. If clogged, rinse it out with warm, soapy water until the unspecified debris has cleared and the drain is as good as new. If cracked, you will need to buy a new one.

PROBLEM 3. YOU HAVE A LEAKING ICE MACHINE

If your refrigerator boasts an ice machine, pull the refrigerator away from the wall and check the water supply line, which will run from the wall into the fridge, via the refrigerator water supply valve. On the other side of the valve should be a small plastic tube that runs into the back of the ice maker. Inspect the supply line and plastic tube for signs of damage that could cause the leak and replace if required, turning the water supply off first to minimize the chances of turning the drip into a torrent. If the line and tube are both in working order, check the valve for leaks and tighten—by hand or using a nice big wrench—if required.

PROBLEM 4. YOU HAVE A FAULTY DOOR SEAL

If you've checked all of the above and you are still having no luck, that only leaves the door seal—or gasket—around the door to check. This is slightly more involved, but not much. Before performing the following steps make sure the gasket is clean—they tend to accumulate grot over time, which needs to be cleaned off every so often with soapy water to ensure a tight seal.

Step 1. If the seal itself appears to be faulty, check that the refrigerator isn't leaning forward, due to a sloping floor. If this happens, the door may not close as tightly as you need, so extend the front legs to compensate and find the balance you need—access to the legs is almost always through the base panel at the front, where you'll find a hinge held in place by one or more screws.

Step 2. Unscrew these, adjust the angle of the hinge to the correct angle, and re-tighten the screws—though to achieve this, you'll need someone to push the fridge back slightly while you work, plus a hearty dollop of WD-40 if the screws are tight.

Step 3. However, check also that the seal hasn't become cracked and, as a result, loose, for this happens over time and allows air in and out of the fridge. To test, hold a bank note of your choice in the fridge, closing the door on it so that half is inside and the other half out. Then, pull the note from the door—a healthy seal will grip it so that you feel resistance. A spent seal will put up little resistance or, if it's really spent, already have allowed the note to fall to the floor. Repeat the test around the entire length of the seal to determine if it needs to be replaced. If it does, you will need to call in a qualified expert to sort it out.

How to... Fix a Faulty Freezer

The biggest and most common problem with the household freezer is that the temperature plays silly buggers. By its very nature a freezer should be freezing cold; otherwise, your big hunks of meat will begin to thaw before you need them and your Sunday roast will be ruined. So if yours isn't freezing food properly, check the following:

CHECK 1. THE POWER SUPPLY
The most basic problem of all is that the freezer is not receiving any power. If in doubt, plug a healthy kettle into the power source to see if it works. If the power source is not working, check the fuse or circuit breaker and reset if they've blown before moving onto Check 2.

CHECK 2. THE THERMOSTAT
Locate the thermostat and switch it to a colder setting (although if you have the opposite problem—the innards

have become overly frozen—turn the temperature up instead of down). If this doesn't work, the controls are probably faulty and will need to be replaced by a qualified professional. If it's not the thermostat, however, try:

CHECK 3. THE DEFROST TIMER

When working properly, this will regulate the defrost cycle and keep things ticking over nicely. When broken, it won't, and you'll end up with an Ice-Age interior or defrosting food. The timer is often located behind the freezer's front grill, but refer to your manual to be sure and unplug the freezer before you go tinkering and risk an electrical shock. To test if the timer is working as it should, locate the "advance screw" on the underside and turn it clockwise until it clicks. This advances the timer to the next mode, i.e., from "cooling" mode to "defrost," or vice-versa. If it doesn't advance again to the next mode within thirty-five minutes or so, the timer is faulty and will need replacing. By an expert, sadly. But if it's not the defrost timer...

CHECK 4. THE CONDENSER COILS

A buildup of dust or debris on the condenser coils can play havoc with the temperature. Turn the freezer off, locate said coils—they are usually the thin, coiled wires on the back or at the front of the freezer, covered by a removable panel—and run a cloth/vacuum cleaner gently over them to remove any grime.

CHECK 5. THE DOOR

Check that the door is closing snugly and sealing as it should. If it's not, air will be traveling in and out of the fridge and causing your problem. Refer to the refrigerator seal details on pages 91–92 for advice; the same rules apply.

CHECK 6. HOME HELP

Unfortunately, if none of the above provide the answer, your freezer is broken and you'll need to call in a qualified expert.

KITCHEN CONUNDRUMS

4

Cracked plates, broken glassware, the knives that were once so dangerously sharp they could chop the head clean off a chicken in one swipe but now struggle to cut through water thanks to all the thwacking and bashing you've subjected them to: These are all-too-common kitchen complaints that can put the brakes on your Jamie Oliver-style antics. But here are some rescue remedies to sort out these everyday annoyances.

How to... Fix a Broken Plate

If you're a fat-fingered fool, or Greek, or both, broken plates will be a common complaint in your household. Damage can range from piffling little chips and unsightly cracks, right up to proper breakages that would usually signal the end of your crockery. But it needn't be that way, as most breaks can be fixed very easily using just a little lateral thinking (and a tube of epoxy resin). How you fix the plate depends on the damage inflicted, so let's take it in order of severity.

A CHIPPED PLATE

A chip can be easily ignored; however, left untreated, a chip can very quickly lead to a crack, which can lead to a break. So the lesson here: Fix your chips and nicks before they escalate. The key is to invest in a tube of clear epoxy resin, a glue that will come in two parts: a resin and a hardener. Once you have that, you're ready.

Avoid all quick-bonding glues; otherwise, you'll have to rush to finish the job and will probably mess it up.

Step 1. Squeeze out equal amounts of resin and hardener onto a piece of card and mix the two together until you have a smooth paste. For the mixing, use a toothpick or matchstick or something similar.

Step 2. Even a clear epoxy resin will dry to a yellowy shade, which is no good unless your plate is yellow. So, dip your glue-tipped matchstick into a pot of paint powder that most closely matches the shade of your china, then dab the gluey powder onto the chip. Fill the chip completely and carefully smooth to a fine finish.

Step 3. Allow the resin to dry, then very carefully scrape away any unsightly excess with a razor blade and admire a very simple job well done. Well done.

A CRACKED PLATE

Once a crack appears in a plate, it's only a matter of time before it breaks in two, leaving you scratching your head over how to fix it. The answer to that's on pages 98–99, but you're strongly advised to address the crack before it becomes a break. Luckily, this is very easy indeed:

Step 1. Turn your oven on and prepare to lightly bake the plate. We're talking a *very low heat* here, just high enough to warm the plate through but not cook it. As it warms, your plate should expand ever so slightly and the crack will open up. While the plate is baking, prepare your epoxy resin, following the directions that are outlined above.

Step 2. When the crack has opened up, put on a pair of oven gloves and take the plate out of the oven; then fill the length of the crack with your glue; and clean off any excess by wiping with a cotton ball dipped in nail polish remover.

Step 3. To apply controlled pressure to the crack, stretch a length of masking tape along the full length of the plate to hold it firmly in place. As it cools it will shrink back to its original size, pulling the glue into the crack to form a tight bond.

Step 4. When the plate has cooled completely and the resin dried, remove the masking tape and use a razor blade to carefully scrape away at any excess resin forced out of the crack. If it's a sharp razor blade, do take care.

The same process applies to chips in cups and mugs: bake it, glue it, tape it, done.

THE PLATE HAS BROKEN IN TWO

This fix will only work if it's a clean break. And it will only work if you have just two parts to piece back together, rather than a million little shards (see page 100 for help with this).

Step 1. Make sure that the break is clean and dry before you mix up a dollop of epoxy resin, ensuring the color matches the color of the plate. (See page 97 for details on this.)

Step 2a. Apply the resin to both broken edges of the plate, then push the two pieces firmly together by hand. Hold until they bond, then stretch a length of masking tape along the join to keep the plate together. Set the plate aside and leave to dry for twenty-four hours.

Or...

Step 2b. An alternative method here is to fill a pan with sand and place one half of the broken plate in the sand, so the broken edge sits rigid and proud in the sand. Glue both edges and push the two pieces together, as before, but this time attach clothespins at both ends of the join. This will keep the halves in place as they dry. If you're feeling particularly gung-ho, of course, you could always secure the plate with both tape *and* pegs, you crazy maverick, you.

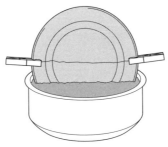

Step 3. Whichever technique you opt for, scrape any excess dried glue off the crack, using a razor blade and taking care not to cut your fingers to ribbons. Wash the plate, and release back into circulation.

THE PLATE HAS SMASHED INTO A THOUSAND PIECES

If you've somehow smashed the plate into several pieces, then your job is considerably trickier but not impossible. Provided you have all the pieces to hand, take another plate of the exact same type and use it as a mould. Place your good plate down on a stable surface as you would for a meal, then place the broken pieces on top, and then accept that you won't be going anywhere for the next few hours and begin to rebuild the broken plate, piece by piece, gluing each edge with epoxy resin and pushing firmly into place. Allow the glue to harden completely before using the plate again. And take more care next time to avoid having to go through this tedious task again.

How to... Fix a Broken Cup Handle

Providing you didn't just drop your favorite cup or mug onto the floor for it to shatter into a million tiny pieces, this is very fixable. If you have the main body of the cup, which from here on in we'll refer to as The Cup, and you have the handle, which we'll refer to as The Handle, then all you need to do is glue the two parts back together. This may well be the easiest fix in the entire book.

Step 1. Wash the parts in hot water and dry completely. You should have two parts in all—one The Handle and one The Cup—and the body of The Cup should have two unpainted circular-ish patches where The Handle had previously been held in place and where you'll need to reattach it.

Step 2. Apply waterproof ceramic glue to the broken surfaces, making sure you have just enough glue, but not so much that it squirts out onto The Cup and your hands when you push them together.

Step 3. Hold the pieces firmly together in a snug fit until the glue dries. Or, if you can't be bothered to hold that position for any length of time, hold just long enough for the glue to bond, then wrap masking tape around The Cup and The Handle to hold it secure while you go away and do something more interesting.

Step 4. Once the mug is completely dry, seal the edges of the crack with a thin bead of waterproof glue to secure it and to keep any grot from penetrating the surface, smoothing it out to a nice clean finish with a popsicle stick. Let this dry, then celebrate a job reasonably done with a nice cup of tea or coffee.

How to... Fix a Broken Glass Stem

The glass in question here is a wine or champagne flute, the type with one of those delicate stems that can snap if you so much as look at them funny. This can be fixed as follows:

Step 1. Purchase a waterproof glass adhesive and apply to both parts of the break, pushing them gently but firmly back together. Hold for a few seconds, just long enough for the parts to bond.

Step 2. With the glass sat on a flat, stable surface, stretch two strips of masking tape around the glass in a cross pattern. This will tighten the pieces and apply the gentle, even pressure the glass needs for the glue to set firm.

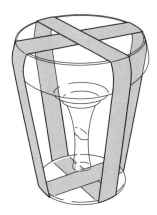

Step 3. Leave the glass long enough for the glue to dry completely (consult the packaging for details), then use a razor blade to gently scrape off any excess glue. Wash the glass before using. And if you spilled wine down your slacks or on the carpet when the glass broke, see page 138 for another miracle cure.

If a glass has any other type of crack or breakage, discard it immediately and buy a new one. There's no point risking it with a glass that may later shatter in your hand or, worse still, your mouth, disfiguring you for life. Take no chances.

How to... Sharpen Blunt Kitchen Knives (the Professional Way)

Unless you paid crazy money for top-end knives endorsed by some frilly celebrity chef, your kitchen blades will have been designed for stain and wear resistance, rather than for keeping a dangerously keen edge. The manufacturers figure you'd prefer it that way, but the result is that the more you use your knives the blunter they become.

To compensate for this, most manufacturers kindly leave the steel slightly soft, making the knives easy to sharpen at home, providing you have a sharpening steel i.e., the long pointy steel thing that professional chefs use to resharpen their blades at great speed. If your knives didn't come with a sharpening steel, you'll need to invest in one now. And because you're not a professional chef and could very easily have your arm off if you start messing about with knives, you'll need to take it slowly and master the basics.

Step 1. Hold the sharpening steel vertically, with the point resting on a work surface, preferably with a towel in between to avoid damage, both to the work surface and the blade, and to give you greater control over the knife.

Step 2. Place the heel of the knife against the edge of the steel, as close to the handle as possible and with the tip pointing upward and away from you at an 18- to 20-degree angle to the steel (see diagram). The top edge of the knife should be held a couple of centimeters closer to the shaft of the sharpening steel than the blade.

Step 3. Pull the edge of the blade across the shaft of the steel and back toward your body in one clean sweeping motion, applying only gentle pressure. The end of the blade should end up close to the point of the steel, at the bottom of the shaft.

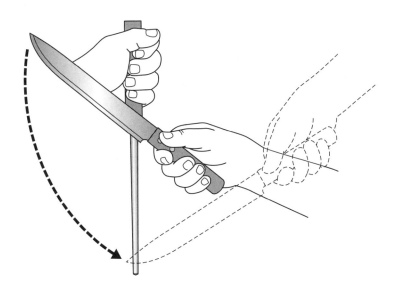

Step 4. Half-a-dozen feisty licks should suffice, then repeat the process on the other side of the blade. To maintain a sharp edge, make sure you resharpen your knives like this before every use.

How to... Sharpen a Can Opener

This couldn't be any easier, hence such a short entry. Make sure the can opener is clean and free from any gunk, then fold a piece of aluminium foil in two and run the entire length of the blade along it. The more you rub, the sharper the blades should become.

How to... Sharpen Scissors

Every kitchen needs at least one pair of scissors with a truly fearsome blade, for cutting through bacon rind and lopping off fish heads. Like all blades, they'll become blunt over time, but this can be fixed. You have two good options here: one mildly fiddly, the other a breeze.

WARNING!
With all blades, make sure they point away from your body. (Or anyone else's for that matter.)

Option 1. The mildly fiddly version involves running the bevelled edge of the blade along a sharpening stone, which is a large stone block most often shaped like a small brick (available from some DIY stores, or over the internet) and in various grits—the finer the grit, the sharper the finish. The stone needs to be lubricated with a light machine oil before use, and you'll need to run the scissor blade from point to pivot—i.e., the bit where the two blades join—with a smooth, steady stroke. Follow the angle of the existing blade as closely as possible, and half-a-dozen lusty strokes should be enough to return it to its former glory. Repeat on the other blade, oiling the stone before you make your first pass of the blade. When you finish with the second blade, open and close the scissors a few times to knock off any rough edges left by the sharpening, and you're finished.

Option 2. The other option is far less fiddly. Purchase and cut through a sheet of coarse sandpaper with your scissors. The more you cut, the more the grit will revive the blades. And for smaller scissors that don't need as much oomph, cut through a sheet of aluminum foil a few times for similar results.

How to... Make Knives and Forks Sparkle Like New

Silver cutlery won't stay sparkling forever, sadly, and if nicks, scratches, and unsightly stains don't get them first, nasty patches of rust often will. Not to worry though, for making jaded cutlery sparkle like new is easy enough, and the following five tips cover most issues.

Tip 1. Restore shine to cutlery by adding a tablespoon of baking soda for every 850 ml of water. Place the solution in a pan, place the silverware in the solution, and let the miracle brew boil up and simmer for five or so minutes. Remove the cutlery, rinse clean, and allow to cool before buffing each piece up to a very pleasing shine.

Tip 2. Should you find unsightly "spotting" on your cutlery, stick the offending article to soak in undiluted white vinegar. Rinse well afterward and the spots should be but a fading memory.

Tip 3. Stubborn stains on silver cutlery can be eradicated by scrubbing them well with a toothbrush and some white toothpaste. You'll need to work up a sweat for this to work, and obviously rinse the cutlery well before using again or your juicy steak will taste of toothpaste.

Tip 4. If you happen to be a big fan of eggs, and your silver spoons are plagued by egg stains, your silver can soon turn black as a result. This is a common occurrence, but the remedy is simple: Rub black areas with salt before washing as normal. And to avoid this in future, clean the cutlery as quickly as possible after use.

Tip 5. Should you find rust on your silverware, just stick the implements into an onion and allow to sit for a while, working them back and forth from time to time to allow the rejuvenating onion juices to work their magic. Finish by washing with soap and water. Alternatively, rub a paste of baking soda and water onto the cutlery for similar results.

How to... Resuscitate a Battered Chopping Board

Years of hacking and thwacking away at your wooden board with sharp knives will eventually leave it with an assortment of unsightly scratches, gouges, and nicks. Not to worry though, because by running a woodworking scraper across the board, you can make it almost as good as new.

Step 1. As a general rule you need to scrape steadily along the board to take off a very thin layer of wood (you will need to refer to the scraper's manual for exact guidance on technique) and with it the scratches and any stains that have built up. Work with the grain to avoid damaging the board, and bend the scraper slightly in the middle for a cleaner scrape.

Step 2. Repeat this as necessary until the board has a fresh, level surface you're happy with.

Step 3. To finish, brush the board with a hearty slug of vegetable oil to season it and protect against future knocks. If brushed with oil every six months or so, your board will last forever and possibly even longer.

ALTERNATIVELY...

To simply remove unsightly stains from a stained wooden chopping board, rather than shave the whole top layer off, coat the board with salt and rub the whole thing with a juicy, pert slice of lemon. Before you can scream "It's a miracle!," the stains should be gone. (Rubbing the juice of lemons or limes onto a board also removes the pungent whiff of garlic and onion.)

How to... Fix a Burnt Pan

You took your eye off your boiling pasta for just one second and now look, your prized pan has a dirty great scorch mark that won't come off no matter how hard you scrub it. Admittedly, a burnt pan won't unduly affect its performance, but it may make your food taste funny, and that's no good. Luckily, you can remedy this by doing the following:

Step 1. Fill the pan with water and add a few spoons of baking soda.

Step 2. Turn up the heat to bring the powdery mix to a boil, and it should magically loosen the burnt bits.

Step 3. Wash as normal and your pan will be as good as new. You can also sprinkle dry soap powder on the pan while it's still hot, drape a cool, damp paper towel over the affected area, and leave to work its magic for an hour. When you come back, the burnt bits will have loosened like a dream (if loose burnt bits are the kind of thing you dream about).

How to... Blitz Rust on a Cast-Iron Pan

As any child could tell you, when iron comes into contact with water and oxygen it will rust—and in double-quick time if salt is present in the water. Everybody knows that, but not everyone knows how to eradicate the rust, even though it's an idiot-proof solution:

Step 1. Pour a good glug of vegetable oil into the pan, then add a similar amount of salt (table or sea, depending on your levels of ponce). Use a scouring pad to work the salty oil into the rust, working up a good sweat, then sloosh the pan out with soapy water, rinse with hot water and dry with a paper towel.

Step 2. To guard against the rust returning (and give the pan its own nonstick coating), you should coat the inside of the pan with vegetable oil, turn it upside down and place on greaseproof paper to catch the drips, and stick in the oven for an hour at around 350ºF (180ºC). Wearing oven gloves, so you do not burn your hands, recoat the pan halfway through. Finally leave to cool and wipe the pan with paper towels before using again.

Step 3. The seasoning process needs to be repeated a number of times for it to become charred and fully nonstick. This may take months to achieve, but it's worth the effort. And after each use, only ever use water and a stiff brush to clean the pan, never hand soap, for you'll only need to remove surface grot, not the layers of oil you've built up. To remove stubborn stains, employ the salt-and-oil method outlined in Step 1.

ALTERNATIVELY... POTATOES

You wouldn't want to be stuck in an elevator with whichever oddball stumbled upon this miraculous remedy for cleaning a rusty pan, but it works. Cut a raw potato in half, and, taking one of the halves, sprinkle it liberally with washing powder. Then apply this to the interior of your rusty pan, using it like you would a scouring pad. Scrub away until the starch somehow magically combines with the cleaning powder to blitz the rust. Don't eat the potato afterwards or you might die.

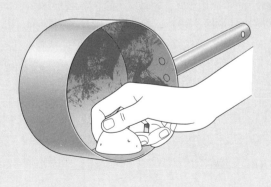

How to... Fix Rusty Baking Dishes

Pour enough cola on the baking dish to cover the rusted area and allow it to soak overnight. This sugar-laden beverage may rot your teeth, but its mysterious cleansing qualities will also eat away at the rust until you can simply wipe it clean.

5

FIXTURES, FURNITURE, AND FURNISHINGS

This section covers the simple fixes you can make around the home; like silencing a squeaking floorboard, fixing a rickety wobbling chair, and removing a variety of heinous stains from your precious shag pile—we're not here to ask you how they got there, just to offer you a solution to get rid of them.

How to... Fix a Squeaking Bed

There's probably a smutty gag to be made here, but let's not plumb the depths just yet. Your bed frame squeaks because parts are rubbing against each other (snigger, hehe, etc.). The simplest solution is to dust baby powder or smear a dab of beeswax on the joints to provide the lubrication the frame needs. This is only ever a temporary solution, mind, and one that must be repeated every time the squeak returns.

For a longer-lasting solution, check and tighten all the screws or fasteners holding the bed together. Better still, take the bed apart and make sure there are washers on the bolts holding the bed together—this will tighten the frame for far longer and ensure a night free from annoying little squeaks.

MATTRESS MAINTENANCE

To make sure the mattress gets even wear and doesn't end up with big body-shaped indents from where you sleep night after night after night, rotate the mattress once a month, and flip it over if you have the strength. This will ensure more even wear and extend its life. And if the bed smells musty, sprinkle baking soda over it and leave to sit for twenty-four hours before vacuuming up. Baking soda will absorb any odors and leave the bed smelling a damn sight better than it did before.

How to... Fix a Wobbly Chair or Table

It's impossible to diagnose your problem with one hundred percent certainty from here, but the legs on that wobbling chair/table are either no longer the same length or the joints have worked themselves loose over time. The following five-step solution should shed a little light:

Step 1. To identify the wobbly leg or legs, place the chair/table upside down with the legs sticking up. Push each leg gently to identify the wobble.

Step 2. Look for any metal brackets holding the legs in place and tighten any bolts on them that need tightening. This may be enough. If it's not, turn over the page...

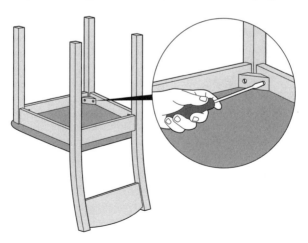

Step 3. Check the bottom of each leg for glides, i.e., the little feet that prevent the chair/table scratching the floor. If one of these feet has gone missing, the table will be off balance. Replace the glide and be done (these are available online).

Step 4. Ensure all joints are secure. Tighten any joint screws and secure with a wood adhesive, keeping the joint in place as it dries by using a corner clamp or a length of rope tied around the joint and another leg of the chair/table.

Step 5. If the problem persists, it may be that through general wear and tear one leg has become shorter than the others. Measure the shortfall and slice a piece of natural cork, a thick piece of felt, or a wedge of cardboard to the correct size and shape. Glue the piece to the base of the short leg, and once it has dried you can use the chair/table as normal.

Alternatively, if you're feeling intrepid, measure each leg to determine if they're all the same length. If one is shorter than the other three, mark the shortest length on the other three legs and sand each of the longer legs until you reach the mark. Use coarse sandpaper to start, then a finer grade paper for the finishing touches.

How to... Fix Squeaky Stairs

When a stair squeaks, it's usually because the two parts it's composed of have loosened over time and are now rubbing against each other every time you step on them. The two rubbing parts are the "tread"—the horizontal piece you place your foot on as you clamber up and down the stairs—and the "riser"—the vertical piece of wood on which the treads sit. See the diagram below and it'll all become clear.

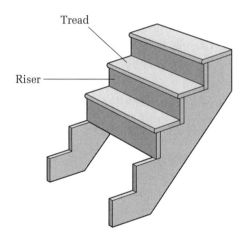

Problem 1. If the squeak is at the front of the stair, the easiest solution is to drive a nail through the tread down into the riser at a 45-degree angle, pulling the two pieces back together in the process. Drive a second nail a couple of inches apart at an opposing 45-degree angle for maximum hold.

Problem 2. If the squeak is at the back of the step, sprinkle talc-free baby powder onto the step and work into the join to lubricate the parts. This, alas, is only a temporary fix and you'll need to repeat every so often, but it should keep the stair from squeaking for a while.

How to... Fix Creaking Floorboards

As wooden floors age, the timber shrinks and warps, causing the floor to separate from the subfloor, i.e., the supporting floor beneath the floorboards. When the two floors separate, the boards will rub against each other every time you walk on them, causing an annoying squeak. To prevent this irritating sound, choose one of the following options:

The Quick Fix: Lubricate the two boards rubbing against each other by dusting the offending section with chalk powder. Sprinkle it between the boards and it should provide temporary lubrication. Stand on the board a few times to work the powder in, then vacuum away the residue and you should be squeak free.

The More Complex Solution: Check if the board end is supported by a joist, i.e., the big wooden support running beneath your floorboards. If there is no joist in place, in time the board will sag. The solution is to take up the board as carefully as possible and screw a wood batten to the side of the joist (see diagram), thereby providing support for the floorboard. Lay the board back on top and reaffix with screws.

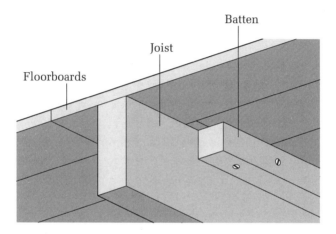

Batten

Joist

Floorboards

The Last Resort: If the previous options do not work, the final solution is to drive a nail into the floor to hold the floor and subfloor together and eradicate the squeak. You'll need to buy several 6D or 8D spiral flooring nails for this, as they're designed to twist into the wood and grip more tightly than plain nails. Walk about until you've located the offending squeak, then drive the nail down at an angle (for better purchase) through the floorboard. Hammer down far enough to make sure the nail is securely into the subfloor. And if nailing through carpet, do exactly the same but fluff up the pile to make sure the nail's head is nicely obscured once you're done.

How to... Bleed a Radiator

A radiator will need bleeding when air enters your central heating. (Luckily, there's no blood involved here, it's just a simple case of turning a nubby little thing until it hisses as the air comes out.) This is a common problem caused by bubbles forming as you heat and cool water and then rising to the highest part of the heating system. These air bubbles will dramatically reduce the amount of heat your radiator emits, causing you to shiver even when you've turned the settings to Full Blast. To test, touch your radiators: If the top is noticeably colder than the bottom when the heating's on, or if it's cool from top to bottom, it needs bleeding. That's the science bit over, here's how you bleed:

Step 1. Turn off the central heating and insert a bleed key into the bleed valve—that's the little screwy nub normally located at the top end of the radiator, or sometimes round the back. Before turning the key, wrap an old rag around it to catch any dirty water, which can spurt out onto your slippers or the carpet.

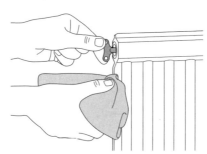

Step 2. Give the bleed valve a half-turn counterclockwise until you hear a hissing sound—don't be overly alarmed, that's just the sound of the air escaping.

Step 3. When the hissing stops, the air has escaped, at which point dirty water should splurge out onto your rag. That's your cue to close the valve by turning it back to its original position—a half-turn clockwise. That's that one bled; now check the other radiators to test if your work is done. If they need bleeding, repeat as above. And be warned that experts suggest you bleed your radiators twice a year, so make a date in your diary.

WARNING!
If bleeding fails, you may have a buildup of corrosion or iron oxide in the system, which will call for the radiators to be taken off the wall and rinsed out with water to remove any gingery sludge water. It may be that the radiator needs replacing, and you'll probably have worked out for yourself that a job of this magnitude is better left to an expert in overalls. Cut your losses and call them sooner rather than later.

How to... Fix Stuck Drawers: Part I

Wooden drawers usually stick or run sluggishly for one of two reasons: Either parts have become loose and so prevent a nice clean pull of the drawer, or the wood has bloated out of shape in particularly humid conditions and made it a struggle every time you try to open the drawer to access your pants. Either way, it's easily fixed.

Step 1. Carefully remove the drawer and check first for obstructions. Loose nails and drawer guides can very often cause drag and make the drawer stick. Remove anything that can be removed by hand (or tighten loose nails if that's the problem), then lubricate the top and bottom edges of the drawer with a good slug of beeswax or plain soap and slide it back in place. That should be enough to get it opening and closing smoothly.

Step 2. If Step 1 doesn't solve the problem, it may be that moisture has permeated the wood, which causes the drawer to swell, making it too fat for its frame. In this case, remove the drawer (which may be a struggle) and gently sand a **very thin layer** of wood from the sides and back. Only ever sand by hand, using a sheet of medium grade 80–100 grit paper; otherwise, you may take off too thick a layer and then the drawer will be too loose to fit, and that would be as bad as it being too tight. Sand a little, then check. Then, if necessary, sand a bit more and check again. Once it fits, lubricate the edges (as in Step 1) and

1) and replace the drawer. And to stop the drawer from swelling in the future, a lick of polyurethane seal or paint to the sides and bottom should suffice.

How to... Fix Stuck Drawers: Part II

If the drawer that is sticking is plastic or metal, rather than wood, it shouldn't stick anywhere near as often because the materials won't change shape when it gets warm. However, if it does, check for obstructions, apply a little lubricant to the parts, and it should run smoothly once more.

How to... Fix a Squeaking Door

A squeaking door is usually caused by friction in the hinge. The squeak won't stop the door from opening and closing, so it's not "broken" as such, but if left untreated, it will rile you to the point of profanity, which is ridiculous when you read how easy it is to fix.

Step 1. Spray each of the hinges with a light lubricant, something like WD-40, for example.

Step 2. If that doesn't kill the squeak stone dead, look for the hinge pins and gently tap the bottom of each with a nail set (this is a short steel punch with a tapered end for striking things, particularly hinge pins). A couple of controlled strikes upward at the bottom of the pin and its top should emerge and stand proud of the hinge. Spray your lubricant onto its steely shaft to coat it, push it back into place with your nail set, and wipe any excess lubricant off the hinge/door. Repeat this process on the other hinges.

Be aware that neither of the above fixes is a permanent solution and you will have to go through this routine the next time the squeak pipes up.

How to... Fix Loose Door Hinges

Any door that hangs heavily on its hinges may eventually end up hanging at a slightly wonky angle, because the weight causes the screws holding the hinges in place to work themselves loose. When that happens, the door sags and no longer fits comfortably in its frame.

Luckily, you could fix this one in your sleep: All you need to do is prop the sagging end of the door up with newspapers so it appears level, then tighten the hinge screws and watch as the hinge and door realign themselves. You could probably have guessed that much yourself, of course, but what happens if tightening doesn't seem to work? Good question. Well then, you'll need to check the screw holes themselves. Often, the screws will turn but won't tighten—which suggests that the screw holes have become worn down and stripped over time, providing no grip for the screw. This fix is more complicated than simply tightening the screws, but not much.

Step 1. Locate the defective screw hole or holes, then remove the screws so that you can take the door off the hinges. Take the door off the hinges, putting those screws safely on one side and leaning the door against something solid.

Step 2. Plug the stripped hole with toothpicks or matchsticks slathered in wood glue. Push these into the hole, let the glue dry, and then use a hacksaw to trim any ends that stand out of the hole, and sand the edges of the hole clean for good measure.

Step 3. Attach the door using all the other fully functioning screw holes first, then carefully drill a pilot hole (i.e., a smaller, exploratory hole) through the toothpick/matchstick hole and carefully drill home the last screw. The toothpicks/matchsticks should provide enough purchase to tighten the door hinge and hold it in place for a good while longer.

ALTERNATIVE AILMENTS

Humid weather can cause some wooden doors (particularly interior) to bloat out of shape, making them too fat for their frames and impossible to shut. In simple cases, rubbing a bar of wet soap over the affected edge can often provide enough lubrication for the door to fit back into its frame. Alternatively, rub a sanding block around the door to trim it down by millimeters. To trim any further, you'll need to have the door planed down until it fits the frame again—a job best left to an expert who knows what they're doing.

How to... Fix a Loose Doorknob

Assuming the doorknob is an old-fashioned knob rather than a less troublesome lever, this fix couldn't be much easier. The following applies to doorknobs inside and outside the house.

Step 1. Look on the shaft of the knob and you should find a very small, spring-activated metal piece. Activate this spring, either by hand or by pushing it with a small, flat screwdriver, and it should click loose to release the doorknob.

Step 2. Pull the doorknob off and then remove the brass or chrome trim plate that sits beneath it. You should now find several screws that hold the doorknob in place—if the knob is wobbling, then the screws will have worked themselves quite loose, though they should still be sitting in their screw holes. Tighten each of the nuts and the doorknob should become better seated.

Step 3. Replace the trim plate, then push the doorknob back into place. And that's about the long and short of it—your wobbling knob should be a thing of the past.

How to... Fix a Sticking Lock

If your key becomes difficult to insert into the lock, or it goes in but won't turn without a struggle, the internal bits will almost certainly need to be lubricated. Graphite powder is your best bet here as it's odorless and designed to stay on the lock, rather than coming off on the key and then on your hands and then all down your pants. Once you've invested in a pot, it's a simple two-step solution.

Step 1. Work a small amount of powder around and into the keyhole. Insert your key and turn it several times to work the graphite into the lock.

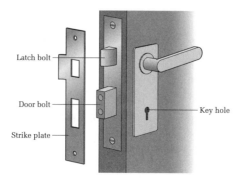

Step 2. While you're there, work more powder onto the door bolt. Close the door and turn the key, which in turn will turn the bolt, which in turn will work the graphite into the strike plate (see diagram), which in turn will make you happy that your lock works as it should again.

How to... Fix Scratched Windows

A pane of glass that's picked up a few cosmetic scratches and nicks along the way needn't be replaced; that would be a gross overreaction and a waste of your time and money. Instead, you can fix the scratch by applying a dab of white toothpaste to completely cover and fill the scratch, then gently scrape any excess off with a razor blade. Allow the toothpaste to dry before gently rubbing it in with a soft clean cloth, working in a small circular motion. Buff until the toothpaste has gone and it will have taken the scratch with it (or so it seems—in reality, the abrasives in the toothpaste will have gently smoothed the scratch out).

As a general rule, if you run your fingernail across the glass and it catches on the scratch, it's too deep to fix. If this is the case, seek expert help as soon as possible, before it comes crashing in on you.

How to... Fill a Gouge in Wooden Furniture

If the piece of furniture in question has a painted finish, this fix is a walk in the park. In fact, it's a walk in the park with a nice picnic and an ice cream.

Step 1. Clean away any debris from the affected area, make sure it's bone dry, then slightly overfill the gouge with wood putty. Give the putty a good twenty-four hours to dry.

Step 2. Sand the excess putty down to a level finish using 200-grit sandpaper. Wrap the paper around a block of wood to make the sanding motion—and your life—easier, then paint in the appropriate shade to finish and you're done. A bloody breeze.

However, if the wooden furniture has a clear finish, then the job becomes a bit more complicated.

Step 1. Clean the affected area and apply the putty, as outlined in Step 1, but then apply five splodges of test putty to a scrap of wood.

Step 2. Wait twenty-four hours, then sand the putty level, as before. However, to ensure you end up with a matching finish, buy a pot of stain that is slightly darker than the wood's finish and a bottle of paint thinner. In four separate containers, mix the stain and paint thinner in ratios of 8:1, 4:1, 2:1, and 1:1, then use a clean, dry rag to apply each mix to the splodge of test putty you prepared yesterday in Step 1. On the fifth splodge of putty, apply the stain neat.

Step 3. Purchase a wipe-on gloss varnish that matches your furniture's original finish. Apply to each test splodge with another clean rag and, almost immediately, you'll see the best match. Mix up a final batch of the correct ratio of stain and thinner, apply to the putty on the furniture, and varnish to finish.

QUICK FIX
A less conventional solution to the gouge problem involves rubbing the gouge in a gentle circular motion with a plump, shelled walnut and watch as its natural oils magically fill the imperfection. Rub, leave the gouge to

rest, then repeat to build up a second layer. Then repeat again and again until the gouge is filled. Finally, buff it up with a soft cloth to finish and the gouge should be gone, or certainly far less visible. This only works on a shallow-ish gouge, of course. Or at least, it's only worth attempting on a shallow gouge, as a massive gouge will take hours to fill and would be better off with the fix suggested on pages 131–132.

How to... Fix Blistering Paint

If you opted to give the walls of your house a lick of paint rather than wallpapering them, you may find the paint begins to play up after a while. Most commonly, it will begin to blister, and while this looks shabby, it's nothing to get overly worried about as it can be very easily fixed.

THE PROBLEM

Blistering paint will show up as patches of air bubbles on your wall, caused by a loss of adhesion. It's caused by excess moisture—either the wall was damp when you painted it, or humid conditions after you painted are now causing a negative reaction, or moisture is seeping through the exterior walls. If it's the latter, you may need to call an expert to fix a bigger problem than mere blistering, but it's worth trying the remedy first.

THE REMEDY

The solution is to gently scrape away the blistering, using a paint scraper, then dry the surface and sand it clean.

Prime the surface, then repaint with a top-end acrylic water-based interior paint to ensure you avoid the blisters returning. Annoyingly, if the paint you apply dries a different shade, you'll have no choice but to paint the whole wall—punishment for cutting corners in the first instance.

ALTERNATIVE AILMENTS—
CRACKING OR FLAKING PAINT

Unassuming hairline cracks along the wall can often end up with dry paint flaking off, leaving bare patches. This is the price you pay for either (a) using cheap, low-grade paint with poor adhesion and flexibility, (b) spreading your paint too thinly like a corner-cutting tightwad, or (c) painting straight onto an unprimed surface like a lazy sod. Scrape away the flaking paint, apply a good quality primer, then finish with a good quality top coat. This should be enough to stop the problem recurring.

How to... Repair Damaged Plaster

A dirty great crack appearing on your living room wall doesn't necessarily mean your house is falling down*; it could simply be a sign of the house "settling" in its foundation, particularly if it's an older house. Of course it may also be a sign that some clumsy clown has knocked the wall with an implement, causing a crack (or hole) to appear. Either way, the solution to this problem remains the same four steps below:

Step 1. Invest in a tub of ready-mixed plaster from your local DIY store and go home, making certain you pay before leaving the premises.

Step 2. Once home, use a small chisel and hammer to chip away at any loose and cracked plaster until you have a firm surface to work with. Brush away any loose debris with a soft cloth.

Step 3. Dry walls can be thirsty beasts, and when you apply plaster, the wall will suck up the moisture and leave the mix dry. So, to buy yourself extra time to work with, dampen the wall with water—use a paintbrush and tap water or a water spray—but make sure you don't saturate it.

*Although it might mean your house is falling down. If you suspect it is, or the crack appears too deep and too long to fill, seek expert help as soon as possible.

Step 4. If you want to be professional, purchase a builder's plaster board and apply the plaster to the crack using a plaster filler or trowel. And if you want to be really professional, pour yourself a mug of undrinkably strong tea to slurp noisily as you work. If it's a deep crack, you will have to build up the filler in stages, leaving it to dry between each application. And if the plaster begins to harden too quickly, dampen it again with your water and brush.

Step 5. When you reach the surface, the filler should sit above the surrounding plaster. Use a wet filling knife to level it off, using a gentle sweeping motion and aiming for a nice smooth finish. Leave to dry, then paint the crack with a paint that matches and your work is done.

How to... Eradicate Carpet Stains

No matter how much care you take, no matter how steady your hand, eventually, inevitably, a dirty great stain will blot your lovely shagpile. Let out your frustration with a good swear, then set about eradicating the stain. Luckily, most can be removed with a combination of cheap household goods and a good dollop of common sense.

WARNING!

For any tip in this section that suggests rubbing a solution onto your carpet, always make sure you exercise a little caution. Before attacking the stain, check on a hidden section of carpet (preferably an off-cut) that nobody will ever see to make sure the solution does not melt the fibers or lift its color. If this happens and you fear you'll only make things worse, consult an expert. If you are happy to proceed, make sure you use a clean, white cloth and blot at the stain, not rub and smear it, for very obvious reasons.

The following are what you might call the Classic Stains:

Grease: If you dropped another pork chop on the carpet while gawking at the TV, sprinkle baking soda over the stain and leave overnight before vacuuming.

Chewing Gum: Attempt to pull sticky gum off your carpet and you'll only succeed in smearing it over a wider area, exacerbating your problem. The trick is to freeze the gum, so it turns brittle and snaps off easily. So, take an ice cube and rub it over the chewing gum to harden it. Wait until it's firmed up nicely, then scrape it away very gently indeed so as not to damage the carpet.

Tea & Coffee: Either mix one teaspoon of clear, mild detergent with one cup of lukewarm water, or mix a cup of 2/3 warm water and 1/3 white vinegar, or just use soda water instead, if you're pushed for time. Sponge your chosen solution on and then blot it with a clean white cloth or paper towels. Finally, blot on clean, lukewarm water to disperse any last lingering signs of your hot beverage. Repeat as necessary. Leave to dry naturally. Rejoice!

Booze #1. Wine: White wine is a breeze: Blot out and sponge the area with soapy water.

Red wine's a pain by comparison and needs to be treated ASAP, if not sooner, otherwise it turns purple and becomes even harder to get rid of. Your best bet is to open a bottle of white wine and pour that straight onto the red stain. Dampen with cold water, then blot, and the red wine should magically disappear. If you have no white wine, simply pour salt straight onto the stain to cover it. The salt will suck the red wine out. Let it dry fully before vacuuming away.

Booze #2. Beer: Act fast and apply a warm water and detergent mix and let it stand for five minutes—most ales should lift very easily. Darker beer and stains allowed to dry are generally tougher to remove but will come out by rubbing glycerine into the stain to loosen, then soaking in a warm-water-and-borax solution and rinsing thoroughly.

Booze #3. Spirits: For everything else that's not wine or beer but is still capable of making you fall down spouting nonsense if drunk to excess, rinse the stain with cold water, apply a liquid detergent, and leave for five minutes. Rinse thoroughly to finish, repeating if necessary. If the stain is stubborn, just leave it to soak for longer.

Mud: Several options here:

Option 1. Apply liquid detergent to the mud, having allowed it to dry first, then blot with a damp, clean white cloth. Vinegar added to the detergent is an optional extra. Or...

Option 2. Squirt white shaving foam to the stain, let it sit for a few minutes, and then blot up with a plain white kitchen towel. Or...

Option 3. Make everyone leave their shoes at the front door in future.

All Other Stains: There is no one-solution-fits-all for stains; if there had been, you'd have stopped reading this section a while ago. However, there are at least two simple solutions that will work on many unsightly marks. The first involves half a cup of white vinegar to one-and-a-half cups of tepid water, mixed and applied to the stain. Let it stand for a few minutes before removing with a damp, clean cloth and repeat if required until the stain has gone. Alternatively, one teaspoon of mild detergent mixed into lukewarm water and applied in the same manner works just as well.

How to... Save an Ailing Carpet

Here are several very simple solutions for several very common carpet ailments, listed in no particular order of importance:

1. REJUVENATE A SHABBY CARPET

It's old and faded and has clearly seen better days, but you can get a few more years out of it yet by sprinkling salt over any dull areas and leaving it to stand for an hour. When you vacuum it off, the carpet will have perked up no end.

2. REPAIR LOOSE CARPET THREADS

Threads will work themselves loose over a period of time, but this is nothing to worry about. Don't yank the thread out, as you risk the whole carpet unravelling before your disbelieving eyes. Far better to cut the pesky thread down to size, using nothing more advanced than a pair of sharp scissors. Trim it down until it falls in line with the rest of the pile. No one will ever know.

3. ERADICATE FURNITURE DENTS ON CARPETS

Heavy furniture left standing in one place for any period of time will leave a carpet dent, which will only be visible when you move the furniture round. Never moving the furniture around would be the obvious answer here, but if you have to and are then left with unsightly marks...

If it's a small dent: hold a steam iron 6 inches (15 cm) above it until the carpet becomes moist, then work the fibers back and forth with the edge of a coin.

Alternatively, place an ice cube on the dent and wait for it to melt. Miraculously, this will encourage the carpet to melt the dent away, but you will need to sponge up the resultant water.

If it's a deep dent: dampen a tea towel/bath towel (depending on the size of the dent) and lay it over the indentation. Apply very gentle pressure with an iron on the wool or cotton setting, then leave the towel in place until it's dry. The heat and moisture combined should miraculously lift the dent. If the dent remains despite your best efforts, you'll need the services of an expert.

4. REPAIR CARPET BURNS

It's normally cigarette ash, of course, so after erecting "No Smoking" signs about the house, your next task is to determine which approach to take:

Approach 1. If the burn isn't too deep, you should be able to get away with simply trimming or shaving off the charred tips of the carpet fibers with scissors or a razor. The slightly shorter length fibers will never be noticed by the human eye.

Approach 2. If it's a deeper burn, find a patch of carpet that visitors will never see—an off-cut or a piece hidden away in a cupboard—and use a pair of tweezers to pull out a few strands. Pluck enough of them so that now, when you roll them together in the palm of your hand, you have a ball big enough to fit the shape of your burn mark. Apply a dollop of carpet adhesive to the hole or mark and press the fiber-fuzz into place. Weigh it down by placing a piece of paper and a big weighty tome (a dictionary, for example) on top and leave to dry. Finally, to finish, walk over it a few times to blend it in as best you can.

6

BATHROOM BUSINESS

You turn on the tap or the shower one fine morning and... oh balls... nothing's coming out. No water, no nothing. You flush the toilet and the waste matter you just deposited refuses to budge. Or, worse still, instead of swooshing down the pan it rises up, up, and over the brim of your toilet, sending a sewage tsunami flooding across your floor. Things break all too easily in the bathroom, but most problems can very easily be remedied and catastrophes averted by following some very simple advice, as outlined in this section.

How to... Unblock a Toilet

If every time you flush the toilet the water level rises almost to the pan rim then drains painfully slowly, you almost certainly have a blockage. Long-term, you may need to reevaluate your diet, but for now the important thing is isolating the blockage and removing it. It will usually be in the pan outlet or in the drain it discharges into—either way, the blockage can be removed by forcing the water down the toilet to dislodge it.

Don't make the mistake of flushing the toilet repeatedly in an attempt to clear it—that will merely send dirty water up and over the rim of the toilet and all over your bathroom floor. The tried-and-trusted solution is to invest in a big plunger, then do as follows:

Step 1. Scoop out any excess water into a bucket, then take your plunger and press it down firmly into the toilet as far as it will go and then pull it slowly upward, but not out of the pan—the rubber head should stay in place as you now push down and then up, then down and then up, and repeat until, after a few goes, you hear water draining down the pipes.

Step 2. When the blockage has been dispersed, the water level should drop to normal. Flush to see if it's cleared properly. If it rises high again, repeat the process outlined above until it drops. And if it doesn't drop, admit defeat and begrudgingly call in a plumber.

How to... Fix a Toilet that Won't Flush

There are several fiddly parts inside the cistern (the box above the toilet seat, which controls the amount of water in the toilet) that can bugger up and prevent the flush mechanism from performing properly, leaving you with a toilet full of waste product and a headache. Luckily, three common causes can be fixed very easily without you having to call out a plumber.

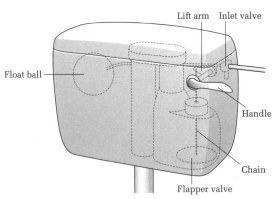

Lift arm   Inlet valve

Float ball

Handle

Chain

Flapper valve

Check 1. The Float Ball

As the name suggests, this is the ball that floats on the water inside the cistern, controlling the level of water in the tank; it's a big ball, you can't miss it. A working cistern should contain enough water for the ball to sit near the top, which in turn extends the float rod (this is the rod attached to the ball) so that it pushes against the inlet valve (see diagram on page 145), which shuts off water coming into the cistern. If there is no water present, the ball may not be rising as it should. Check in case the ball has become misaligned and is touching the sides of the cistern, as this could stop it from rising. If this is the case, carefully bend the float rod by hand until it rises cleanly again. Also check that the rod and the ball are in working order—if either appear damaged, they'll need to be replaced. This, alas, is too fiddly for an amateur and should be left to an expert.

Check 2. The Handle

A common problem is that the handle is too loose to activate the flush. This happens because the retaining nut on the opposite side of the toilet cistern to the handle has worked itself loose. To check, lift the cistern lid off and turn the offending nut with a wrench until it's secure but not too tight.

Conversely, if the handle is stiff and won't push down smoothly to flush, the nut may have become coated in limescale. Brush the nut with white vinegar to loosen the buildup and make the handle work like new.

Check 3. The Chain

The final check is the chain (as illustrated on page 145), which flushes the toilet and which on a fully function-ing lavatory should run from the lift arm down to the flapper valve at the bottom of the tank. There needs to be sufficient slack in the chain for the toilet to be able to flush properly. Check by hand that you can pull the chain up by about half an inch (1 cm) before it begins to lift the flapper valve. If it's too loose or too tight, you won't be able to do this, so adjust accordingly by unhooking the chain and setting it on a different hole. You may need to experiment until you find the right tension, but when the alternative is feces floating across your floor, it's well worth the effort.

How to... Fix a Dripping Tap

You can live with the odd drip; that's quite normal and nothing to worry about. It's when it builds from the odd drip into an incessant drip... drip... drip-drip-effing-drip that it becomes a problem. Not only will you lose sleep and money, because you're paying for every last drip that disappears down the plug hole, but over time drips will leave dirty stains on your sink or bath. So, a quick fix:

The general rule is that if water drips from the spout, the problem is caused by the washer; if it drips from the handle, it's the O-ring. Observe, and then follow the appropriate tips.

WARNING!

To avoid being sprayed in the face in farcical fashion, turn the water supply off before you start tinkering with the taps, either at the isolating valves under the sink or at the main stopcock. Then turn on the tap in question to remove any water lurking in the pipes. When it runs dry, turn it off and put the plug in to catch any small fiddly parts you'll inevitably drop down the plug hole.

PROBLEM 1. A DRIP FROM THE SPOUT

The washer is the small circular rubber part inside the tap, designed to provide a seal. The fact it's dripping suggests the washer is faulty and needs to be replaced. Visit a DIY store and buy a replacement washer; then you're ready.

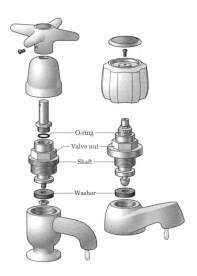

Step 1. Remove the top of the tap, which almost always involves unscrewing a nut that holds it in place. On older taps the screw will be visible on the shaft of the tap; on modern taps it will normally be concealed under the hot (red) and cold (blue) indicators, which can be very easily pried off using a small flat-head screwdriver. Remove the screw and the top should pull off without much effort.

Step 2. Next, use a wrench to remove the main valve nut (see diagram). As you turn the wrench, hold the tap spout firmly to stop the body of the tap turning, rather than the nut. Turning the tap can damage the workings below and cause leaks in the pipes, which you don't want. To protect the nut against scratches while turning, place a cloth between nut and wrench as you turn.

Step 3. Pull out the shaft (see diagram) and at the bottom you'll see the washer, a small circular rubber piece. If it pulls straight off, pull it straight off. If it has a retaining nut, unscrew this first and then pull it off. Push the new washer in—which will need to be the exact same dimensions as the old one—and then reverse the instructions above to screw the headgear back on to the tap, taking care not to overtighten. The tap should now drip no more.

PROBLEM 2. A DRIP FROM THE HANDLE

If the tap leaks from the handle, the most likely cause is a defective O-ring. This rubber ring lives toward the top of the tap's shaft (see diagram). Over time the ring will weaken, allowing water to escape from the tap. To replace it, follow Steps 1, 2, and 3, but rather than removing and replacing the washer, gently ease off the O-ring with a small screwdriver instead, smear the replacement ring with grease to make it last longer than the old one, then push back into place and reassemble the tap by reversing Steps 1–3 of Problem 1.

How to... Fix a Tap That Won't Turn

Hard water* running through your taps can cause a buildup of limescale, which at worst will paralyze the internal bits and make turning the water on and off an ever-increasing pain in the ass, and at best ensure that what was once a mighty torrent of water soon becomes a pathetic trickle. So it needs to be addressed, which luckily for you is very easy indeed.

Step 1. Turn off the water supply and remove the tap's cover or handle, then pull out the shaft, following Steps 1 and 2 of Problem 1 on pages 149–150.

Step 2. Take a small, soft brush (one small and flexible enough to get into the shaft's nooks and crannies) and dip it in vinegar and gently use it to work away at the shaft to remove any limescale.

Step 3. That's all there is to it. You could pat the shaft dry with paper towels if you want to look really busy, but it's going to get wet when it goes back inside the tap so

* Hard water has a higher mineral content (calcium and magnesium) than soft water. Because of those minerals, hard water can often leave mineral deposits in your pipes and kettle, otherwise known as limescale, which will need to be cleared regularly for things to function as they should.

there's very little point. Piece it all back together, reversing the steps you just followed to remove the shaft, and you're all done. Well done.

How to... Unblock Clogged Sinks

If your sink becomes clogged up with dirt and debris, it will start to back up, stink, then spill water out onto your floor. This will ruin your floor and possibly your socks or your slippers, so you'll need to act early to avoid it reaching that stage. Unblocking sinks can be broken down into three stages, as follows:

STAGE 1. THE LIQUID SOLUTION

You could very easily invest in one of the many specialist drain-cleaning products on the market, but the chemicals involved in some of them have been known to corrode pipes. A better, more natural alternative is to pour boiling water down the drain—a simple shock tactic that often proves sufficient.

For more dramatic results, sprinkle one cup of baking soda down the drain, add one cup of white vinegar, and then stand back and enjoy the chemical reaction. When the fizzing's died down, rinse with piping hot water. Repeat as many times as necessary. If that fails, consider Stage 2.

STAGE 2. THE BIG PLUNGER

If the blockage can't be flushed out using water, you'll need to use suction instead, using a big rubber plunger they sell in all good DIY and hardware stores. Fill the sink with two or three inches of water, then slather a thick slug of petroleum jelly around the edge of the plunger to increase suction and plunge it up and down briskly over the hole. You should not be aiming to push the clog farther down the pipe, but to establish a vacuum that will pull it out. Pause to evaluate every so often, and if the blockage has not cleared, keep plunging until it does so. When it is finally clear, pour boiling water down the sink to flush away any last stubborn blockages.

STAGE 3. THE LAST HOPE

If Stages 1 and 2 fail you, cleaning out the P-trap may be your last resort before calling the plumber. The P-trap is that curvy length of plastic that sits out of sight in the cupboard below your sink and can collect debris.

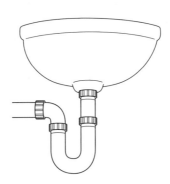

To clean it, first shove a bucket beneath the trap to catch any dirty water, then turn off the water supply to avoid an hilarious soaking. Newer P-traps can be twisted apart by hand; older models will be kept in place with nuts, which will need to be carefully removed with a pair of pliers. Loosen the nuts, then unscrew and remove by hand and put them safely to one side. Remove the P-trap, and let the water it contains drop into your bucket. Rinse the trap out with hot, soapy water to remove any stubborn blockages, then reattach it and tighten the nuts fully.

STAGE 4. ALL HOPE HAS GONE

If none of the above works, curse loudly and call a plumber.

How to... Fix a Trickling Shower

If you turn on the shower and it only coughs up a sorry little dribble of water that wouldn't wet a mouse, chances are the showerhead has become clogged up with your old enemy: limescale, which builds up over time and with frequent usage. This will probably appear as white, powdery buildup around the head's holes and joins and will need to be removed for the shower to work properly again. Here are a couple of suggestions for tackling the problem:

THE EASY OPTION

The simplest solution is to wipe the showerhead thoroughly with a soft cloth liberally dipped in water mixed with a hearty slug of white vinegar. This should soften the limescale, making it easier to wipe away. Push at the holes on the head with a toothpick and it should unblock the blockages. However, as you're pushing the gunk back into the head, the problem is likely to recur sooner rather than later.

THE MORE COMPLICATED ALTERNATIVE

This is a more thorough solution that involves taking off the showerhead and thoroughly cleaning out its insides. It's more complicated but yields far better long-term results.

Step 1. To protect the showerhead from damage, wrap masking tape around the head coupling (i.e., where the showerhead connects to the pipe), then use pliers to gently unscrew and remove the showerhead.

Step 2. Gently pry the head apart by hand, using a blunt knife to open it up along the seal. Place both parts (and any interior pieces) of the head into a bucket containing a mix of one part water to three parts white vinegar and leave them to soak for twenty-four hours. The vinegar in the mix will dissolve the limescale.

Step 3. A day later, take a toothpick or cocktail stick and poke it through the holes on the showerhead to clear any remaining limescale.

Step 4. Scrub the showerhead inside and out with an old toothbrush until every last trace of limescale has gone, then rinse the parts in cold water and dry thoroughly.

Step 5. Piece the head and pipe back together and turn on the shower. And what was a pitiful trickle should now be a torrent of biblical proportions.

How to... Fix a Leaking Shower

If you have already cleaned the showerhead (see pages 154–155) and the leak persists, it's more likely that your problem is due to a defective washer, which you will find located where the pipe screws into the showerhead. When it's working properly, the washer provides a seal to keep the water in. If it's cracked or damaged, it provides no seal at all, and water spills out everywhere. These steps should have it fixed in a jiffy:

Step 1. Use pliers to unscrew the showerhead from the outlet pipe, protecting the head from damage by wrapping tape around the section where the head screws onto the outlet piping.

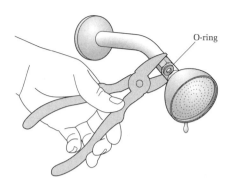

O-ring

Step 2. At the base of the head you'll now see the little O-ring. If the O-ring appears to be damaged or weakened, replace it with a new one, which you can buy from a DIY store.

Step 3. Push the O-ring into the showerhead as far as the lip and screw the showerhead back onto the outlet pipe. Problem almost certainly solved. If not, you know who you'll need to call.

How to... Fix a Cracked Bath

A bath with a crack that goes all the way through its side will leak and leave a puddle of water on the floor, which will cause damp, and potentially make the floor come crashing in on the poor people below. That's the worst-case scenario, of course, but you don't want to risk it. Fixing this is a matter of great urgency, therefore, but should only be attempted if the crack is no more than an inch or two long, and only millimeters wide. For serious cracks any larger than this, seek out expert help or buy a new bath (which may be cheaper). For small cracks, however, the fix is simple enough.

Step 1. Work from the underside of the bath if you have easy access to it; this usually involves removing a panel, but you'll need to assess that yourself. Why work on the underside, you may or may not ask? Good question. Simply because the filler you'll use at Step 2 will be less obvious if applied out of sight on the underside of the bath. So locate the crack and make sure it's clean and dry before you operate.

Step 2. To fill the crack, you have two good options. Either (a) invest in a polyester filler, or (b) invest in a two-part, pliable epoxy repair compound, asking the man in the shop to point you in the right direction. With both options you'll need to apply the filler to the crack, smooth it out with a damp sponge, and leave to dry.

Step 3. When the filler/epoxy is bone dry, sand clean on the visible side of the bath so that it sits flush with the rest of the bath, then cover the filler with the appropriate shade of waterproof glue. And you're done.

For a smaller crack that hasn't yet gone all the way through the bath but may if ignored, skip Step 1 and start at Step 2.

How to... Fix a Cracked Bathroom Tile*

If you can be trusted to use a hammer without smashing anything, repairing a cracked bathroom tile is a breeze.

WARNING!

Broken tiles can be sharp and dangerous. Guard against injuries by wearing safety glasses and gloves when chipping away at broken pieces. And wear some stout shoes too, while you're at it.

Step 1. Before addressing the cracked tile, check if any other tiles around it are damaged by tapping them very gently with the end of a hammer. Any tiles that give off a thinner, more hollow sound are likely to be weak and will need to be removed.

*This fix also applies to any other tiles you may have broken about your house.

Step 2. To remove the tile, first drill a small hole in its center, then insert a chisel into that hole at an angle between the back of the tile and the wall/floor/whatever surface the tile is fixed to. Hammer gently until the tile cracks enough for you to be able to easily chip and then pull out the broken pieces.

Step 3. When the tile has been removed, use a blunt knife to scrape out any old adhesive left behind on the wall. If the adhesive is stubborn, heat the knife's blade over a flame for a few seconds and watch as it cuts through the stubborn gum with ease.

Step 4. Apply a splodge of silicone adhesive to the back of the new tile or the surface you will be fixing it to, giving it a nice even spread. Squeeze the tile into place, using tile spacers or matches to ensure the gaps are even. If the tile doesn't sit flat alongside its neighboring tiles, remove adhesive where required until it does. With the tile in place, clean away any excess glue on the tile face with a damp cloth or sponge, then leave to dry for twenty-four hours.

Step 5. A day later, and not a moment sooner, take a tube of tile grout and pipe it into the gaps around the tile. When the gaps have been filled, use a damp sponge to wipe away any excess and then allow the grout to dry. Finally, buff up the tile with a dry cloth for a truly textbook finish.

GARDEN GUIDANCE

The garden and exterior of your house are veritable minefields of accidents waiting to happen. If it's not the guttering clogging up and sagging low, it'll be the wonky gatepost or the blunt garden tools; or perhaps the mower that won't mow; or those terra-cotta pots with the great big cracks in them. All these troubles and more are outlined as follows, so get your rain boots on and let's get to it.

How to... Fix a Sagging Garden Gate

A garden gate can often sag if it's been built on soil rather than concrete, because the wood sucks up moisture from the earth, which eats into the timber and makes it sag. This will ultimately land the gate in an ugly heap on the ground, possibly bringing down the entire fence too. To avoid this unpleasant scenario, you need to realign the gatepost at the first sign of sagging. This is fairly easy.

Step 1. Tighten any screws on show with the appropriate screwdriver, and if you're lucky, this can often be enough to bring the whole gate back into line and save you the bother of moving on to Step 2.

Step 2. If Step 1 doesn't work, you'll need to whip out a spirit level and check that the gatepost stands up perfectly straight. If it is sagging, pull the post back to the middle and dig away at the soil on the side on which it sagged—so if it leaned left as you look, dig up the soil to the left of the post, going 10–20 inches (25–50 cm) deep and six or so inches (15 cm) wide.

Step 3. The soil is too weak to hold the weight of the post, hence the sagging, and therefore needs to be replaced with fine gravel. So with the gatepost standing bolt upright (and checked using your spirit level), fill the excavated hole around the base of the post with gravel, packing it in to hold it firmly in place.

Step 4. Take a long, thin wooden wedge, about 6 inches (15 cm) long, and place the flat edge against the gatepost, between the post and the gravel. Then take a hammer and drive the wedge down until its top end sits neatly at ground level. The wedge offers greater resistance against the gate post sagging again and will hold it in place for longer.

Step 5. Finally, pack more gravel in around the top of the wedge to bury it out of sight, and you should be all done. If, after all that, the gate continues to sag, you might want to consider replacing the gravel option with concrete, although that's a big job for a proper tradesman, sadly.

How to... Fix a Blocked Gutter

Old leaves can very easily flutter down into your gutter and cause blockages that leave it all saggy and out of shape. You might think that if you can't see them then it doesn't much matter, but you'd be wrong. Ignore a sag and it can often cause a leak, and a leak can lead to all sorts of problems both inside and outside your house.

So, to prevent a molehill quickly becoming a mountain, you need to fix a sagging gutter at the earliest opportunity by following these instructions.

WARNING!

There are many heroic ways to meet your maker (rescuing blind orphans from a burning building, for example, or taking a bullet for the Queen), but falling off a ladder while reaching for some leaves is not one of them. So, when using a ladder to reach the guttering, make sure it sits safely on the ground—angled at no more than 75 degrees, planted on flat, stable ground, with a trusted assistant holding it firm and positioned so that you never have to overreach and fall to your death.

Step 1. Unless you have unfeasibly long arms, you'll need to use a ladder to reach the guttering. Once you're up there, remove the blockages by hand and throw them onto the ground or over your neighbor's fence.

Make damn sure you only ever work from the downpipe (the pipe running down from the gutter to the drain) outlet toward the end of the gutter, and never the other way around. Working away from the downpipe ensures you don't push any more debris down it and make the situation worse.

Step 2. Once the gutter is clear, clamber back down the ladder and gently poke away at the foot of the downpipe with a thin implement—a wire coat hanger or a small stick, for example—to remove any blockages. Pull out any gunk by hand.

Step 3. Finally, head back up the ladder with a hose to flush out any stubborn blockages hidden away in the downpipe. Ask your assistant to turn the hose on only when you're in place and not before. Finally, place a piece of gauze over the downpipe hole to prevent leaves from pushing down and causing another blockage in the future.

How to... Sharpen Garden Tools*

WARNING!

Wear protective gloves at all times when dealing with tools—even a dull garden tool can be sharp enough to lop one of your body parts clean off. Also, never, ever place your body parts in the path of any blade, and if it's safer to clamp the tool in a vise before working on it, clamp away.

Over time the blades on your gardening tools will lose their zingy edge, making it much harder to cut through your conifers, dig a big hole, or whatever it is you do out there in your Wellington boots. Also, there's a safety issue here, for the harder you have to push a blunt tool to make it work, the more likely you are to slip with it and slash an arm or a leg off, and that's not ideal.

*NUTS

If the tool has a pivot nut involved—as it may with secateurs and the scissor family of tools—tighten it if required, as a slack nut will often loosen the two blades and result in a loss of bite in the blades. If by tightening the nut the blades give a better cut, you can skip the rest of this entry and fix something else.

So, here are some sharpening instructions to return your tools to good working order. These apply to any tool that features two sharp, scissor-like edges that meet at the bottom of the blades and cut right up to the tip (e.g., secateurs, pruning shears, loppers, grass clippers, etc.) and also to any bludgeoning implement with an edge that has seen better days (e.g., the blades of a spade, a hoe, a big angry axe, etc.). Select your weapon and follow the sharpening process below.

Step 1. Make sure the tool is free of any dirt or grime, washing with soapy water and drying thoroughly if necessary. Filing a filthy blade can cause more damage, so don't be tempted to cut corners here. Also check for signs of rust and remedy before you sharpen (see page 169 for details).

Step 2. In the interests of health and safety, clamp the tool firmly in a vise, then select the right metal file for the job. Files come in various dimensions, and the person behind the counter at the DIY shop should be happy to advise (or at least be willing to wave you in the vague direction of the wrong aisle).

Step 3. Locate the original bevel, a.k.a. The Blade Edge—even blunt tools should have an existing bevel you need to follow. Hold the file firmly at the same angle, which will be between 40 degress and 75 degrees depending on the tool, and make a few smooth, even passes over the blade to sharpen it, moving away from you with each stroke.

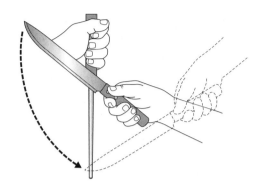

After a dozen or so strokes, you should see clean, sharp metal emerge beneath. Repeat this across the full length of the blade until the sharp edge has returned.

Never file back and forth, as that causes damage, and avoid small, jerky movements or you'll lose the edge.

Step 4. Very lightly sand the back edge of the blade to remove any burrs (the rough, metallic bits left by the filing action). Wipe the blade on both sides with an oily rag (use light machine oil) to protect against rust, dry well, and your tools should be as good as new.

If the blade is clearly damaged, rather than just blunt, none of the above will help you. Discard and replace the tool or accept that you'll need to pay an expert.

How to... Rescue Rusting Tools

Rust weakens tools, eating away like a virus as it spreads into the metal and gnaws away from within. If it's caught and treated early, you can prevent long-term damage.

Step 1. Take a cloth and rub general purpose oil over the rust, then take some steel wool and rub downward at it. If the rust is particularly stubborn, you may have to repeat this step.

Step 2. Alternatively, add Ceylon tea bags to a big vat of boiling water, allow the tea to stew until the water is murky brown, and then submerge the tool in your miracle brew overnight. The tannic acid in the tea will eat away at the rust.

Step 3. Whichever method you choose, when you've finished, take a soft cloth and rub away any remaining rust particles, then wash the tool in warm soapy water and dry thoroughly. And to avoid Steps 1 and 2 in future, dry your tools well after every use and store in a warm, dry environment.

> **WARNING!**
> Ensure that tools with any moving parts are tightened and well oiled every few months; otherwise, they'll rust and seize up. If you're feeling particularly adventurous, very carefully dismantle the tool and oil all the moving parts, but make note of how it came apart so that you can piece it back together again.

How to... Troubleshoot a Faulty Electric Mower

Modern lawn mowers can fail you for any number of reasons, what with them being packed full of complicated little wires, fiddly filters, and assorted whatnots. However, the most common complaint amongst mower users is that the damn thing won't start, no matter how many times you push the button, kick the machine, or swear at it. But fret not, the problem can usually be fixed by counting to ten, and then reading through this troubleshooting guide.

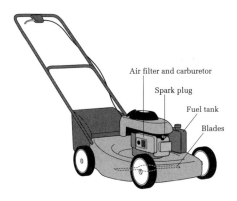

Air filter and carburetor

Spark plug

Fuel tank

Blades

CHECK 1. THE FUEL

Is there any in the mower? If not, go away and fill it with fresh fuel and let's pretend we never had this chat. If there is fuel in the mower but it's old fuel left for months to fester, it will have gone stale, and stale fuel will not start and run a mower, so you'll need to change it. As a rule, always drain the fuel after every mowing season; the easiest way to do this is to run the power until the petrol runs out.

If you suspect water has mixed in with the fuel, which can occur if ice forms on the mower and melts in the tank, then the fuel will need replacing.

CHECK 2. THE CARBURETOR

Petrol left in the engine for any length of time will often evaporate and clog up the mower's carburetor, which in turn will impede the engine. Sadly, repairing the carburetor is a very fiddly fix best left to an expert who knows what they're doing.

CHECK 3. THE AIR FILTER

As a general rule, the filter should be changed every couple of years. Where it sits depends on the model of mower, but as a general rule, follow the fuel hose down from the fuel tank and it will go into the carburetor— your filter should sit beside the carburetor, but refer to your owner's manual if in any doubt. Remove the filter by hand and hold it up to the light. If you can't see light through your filter, it'll need to be cleaned. Warm, soapy water should suffice—simply wash, wipe off any excess oil or grime, leave to dry, and then reinsert the filter. If the filter appears worn or damaged, purchase an exact replacement and carefully insert into the mower.

CHECK 4. THE SPARK PLUG

Without a firing spark plug the motor will not turn over and start, but luckily the plug can be replaced at very little cost. Generally speaking, the plug will sit at the front of your mower, underneath the spark plug wire (but if in any doubt, refer to your owner's manual). Wiggle off the wire by hand and you'll see the spark plug jutting out. This can be extracted using a spark plug socket, rotated until the plug is loose enough to be unscrewed by hand. Once removed, you could always clean the spark plug, but replacing it is far quicker and easier and should guarantee the mower runs efficiently for longer. Replace, tighten first by hand and then with your socket, then replace the wire. You're all fixed.

CHECK 5. THE BLADES

Wet grass can clog the underside of the mower and stop the blades from turning. And if the blades don't turn, the engine often won't start. Remedy this by removing any blockages by (gloved) hand, having unplugged the mower and removed the spark plug wire first (referring to Check 4 for specifics) to prevent your hands from being sliced off in a terrible accident.

CHECK 6. THE BLADES AGAIN

If you somehow damaged the blades during your last mowing session (by hitting a rock or taking the top off a hedgehog), you could have bent them out of shape. If this happens, your mower should still start but will cough, splutter, and shake about all over the shop, because a bent blade will not rotate as the manufacturer intended it to. Most blades can be replaced, providing you have the make and model to show the man in the shop when you purchase a replacement. After that it boils down to four very simple steps:

Step 1. Turn the lawn mower off and leave to cool, then remove the spark plug wire to kill the machine completely.

Step 2. Access the blade compartment by turning over or removing the mowing deck, if the deck removes (see manual). And for the sake of your slacks, make sure all petrol has been removed before turning it over.

Step 3. Don thick gloves and remove debris from the underside of the mower. Then take the correct size socket and loosen the nut that holds the blade in place. With that off you can carefully remove the blade from its spindle.

Step 4. Put the old blade to one side, out of harm's way, then slip the new blade onto the spindle, ensuring it's balanced before reattaching the bolt and tightening.

How to... Fix a Cracked Flower Pot

As any amateur horticulturist will tell you, inclement weather and cold snaps can very easily diddle your plant pots, particularly if they're the delicate terra-cotta sort. You should really store all delicate pots inside when it gets cold, but we're guessing the horse has bolted if you're reading this entry, so here follows a solution for fixing cracks before they turn into breaks:

FOR SMALL POTS...

Step 1. Clean off all dirt and make sure the crack is bone-dry before taking out a tube of silicone caulk.

Step 2. By hand, very gently pry the crack apart, just far enough to squeeze in enough silicone caulk to fill its entire length.

Step 3. Allow the crack to settle back, then tie a length of rope or thick string around the pot to tighten the gap and hold it closed. Or, as an alternative, place the pot in a tub and pack sand tightly around it to push and hold the split together.

Step 4. Leave the rope/string/sand in place until the caulk has dried completely, which could take several hours, ideally overnight. Once dry, remove the rope/string/sand and scrape or sand away any excess caulk for a presentable finish.

FOR LARGE POTS...

Again, you'll need to fill the crack with silicone caulk, as outlined above, but then wrap a length of rust-proof wire around the top and bottom of the pot for extra stability. This can be done as shown on the next page.

Step 1. Drill a very small hole on each side of the crack, about 1 cm away from the crack itself. If it's a long crack, you may need more holes farther down, on either side of the crack.

Step 2. Snip your wire to size (i.e., just large enough to stretch the full circumference of the pot), then thread an end inside one of your drill holes and twist it tightly with pliers to secure it inside the pot.

Step 3. Take the other end of the wire and thread it around the circumference of the pot and into the other hole, twisting with pliers until the crack closes and is held tightly in place. A pedant might look at the pot and remark that you are holding it in place with a length of wire, but most people will never notice and your pot will be as good as new.

How to... Piece Together a Broken Plant Pot

A crack left to grow can often turn into a break, and that's always far, far harder to fix. You should really read pages 174–175 to learn about fixing a crack and nip this one in the bud, but if it's all too late for that and the pot breaks cleanly, and you have all the parts, fixing it is possible with the following instructions.

Step 1. Brush the pieces clean, with a, erm, brush, and make sure all the edges are clean and dry.

Step 2. Apply a waterproof two-part epoxy resin that matches the color of your pot to bond the pieces back together. Wipe away any excess resin from the outside of the pot so it's nice and clean and presentable.

Step 3. Stretch masking tape around the circumference of the pot—top, middle, and bottom—to tighten the joins and leave it to dry overnight. Or, alternatively, stick the pot in a container and pack sand around it to provide the same kind of pressure it needs until the glue dries.

Step 4. When you come back the next morning, remove the tape/sand and use a razor blade to carefully scrape away any dried glue. Stick your soil and plants back in the pot and it should now be as good as new.

If the pot has broken into a thousand tiny pieces, ask yourself if it's really worth the effort of painstakingly piecing the whole thing back together. If the answer is yes, you should really get a hobby. Also, because the pots don't get on with cold weather (especially if they've been repaired), keep them inside during the winter months or any unseasonable cold snaps.

How to... Fix a Torn Garden Umbrella

Garden umbrellas, being made of flimsy canvas or plastic, invite trouble. Often all it takes for them to rip is a violent gust of wind or some boozed-up clown falling into them at a social gathering. Either way, the end result is usually a rip that will need to be fixed.

Providing it's a fairly tidy rip, leaving you with two flapping pieces of umbrella, the easiest remedy is to purchase an iron-on patch sold in all decent hardware stores, haberdashers, and many of those giant supermarkets that have swallowed and spat out all the decent hardware stores and haberdashers. Once you've bought the patch, lay the torn section flat and cut the patch to the appropriate size. Place the patch over the tear on the underside of the umbrella, then iron over to seal it. It really couldn't be easier.

How to... Repair a Hose With a Hole

A hole at either end of your hose is quite normal and nothing to worry about—you'll need a hole at either end for it to work and spurt water about your garden. The problem comes when additional holes—and cracks—appear along the length of the hose, because they will allow the water to leak out. In most cases this is caused by buying a cheap hose with no protective inner lining, so some might say you brought the predicament upon yourself with your tightfisted ways. However, who are we to judge? Instead, here are some tips to help you remedy the situation:

Tip 1. Always attend to small tears or punctures at the first sign of trouble, before they have the chance to become big tears and punctures that are much harder to fix.

Tip 2. A bicycle puncture repair kit can patch up most small holes, providing you read the instructions on the pack or on pages 198–200 very carefully.

Tip 3. Black plastic tape can patch up a tear, providing it's waterproof, applied to a dry hose and wrapped tightly around the hole, with an extra 2.5–5 cm on either side of the hole/crack for good measure.

Tip 4. Alternatively, dry the offending hole thoroughly before applying a splodge of rubber cement over the hole and leave it to dry before using again. Don't apply so much cement that it falls into the hose and causes a blockage inside, though, for very obvious reasons.

Tip 5. However you choose to fix the hose, make sure you do so on a hot, sunny day, when the hose will have had time to warm up and expand. This makes it more malleable and the whole job a damn sight easier. If the sun is not shining, run the hose under a hot tap for a few minutes for similar results.

SPORTS AND LEISURELY PURSUITS

Sport is good for you. That's official. It makes you wheeze and splutter and your cheeks go red, and helps you live longer. But what if your bike's broken, your skateboard is sluggish, and the grip on your tennis racquet's gone? You might be tempted to turn to other leisure pursuits, like fishing, or reading your favorite book. But no! Your rod's in need of repair and your book's falling to pieces. Well, you'd better read on, or you'll spend your free time cursing and going red for all the wrong reasons.

How to... Fix Books

Most basic book repairs are very simple, providing you have at hand a bottle of pH-neutral adhesive (available from all good hardware stores), a sharp knife, and a steady hand. The most common book repairs are detailed here.

REPLACING LOOSE PAGES...

Step 1. Carefully remove the page in question and paint a *very thin* strip of pH-neutral adhesive down the full length of the spine edge of the page, both front and back. The pH-neutral adhesive won't shrink or crack as it dries, and dries clear rather than turning a grim shade of yellow.

Step 2. Turn to the correct page for insertion, weigh down the opposite half of the book so it's secure, then line up the edge of the page farthest from the gutter so that it's in line with the pages that follow, making sure it sits as squarely as possible. Next, hold the page in place with one hand and run a ruler (or similar straight edge) from the outside edge of the page toward the gutter. The ruler will give you a smoother, cleaner finish as you push the edge of the page into place.

Step 3. With the adhesive edge in place, close the book and place a heavy object on top to push down on the page and encourage the adhesive to fix more securely. Finally, when the adhesive has dried, check the alignment of your fixed page. If your alignment's jiggered, as they say in the book business, and the page juts out noticeably, trim the excess down with scissors or a very sharp craft knife to finish.

FIXING A TORN PAGE...

Place a piece of scrap paper beneath the damaged page, to protect the page below from further damage. Lift one side of the tear and brush a coating of pH-neutral adhesive along its inside edge, then another coating along the edge on the opposite side of the tear. Avoid overslathering the glue on as it will only end up on the page, risking an unsightly stain.

Push both edges back down into place so that they lie flat on the scrap paper, wiping away any excess adhesive that does spill out. Place a sheet of wax paper over the page to soak up any further adhesive that spills out and to protect the preceding page, then close the book, place a heavy weight on top of the book, and leave it to dry. When it dries, remove the paper inserts and you're done.

REATTACHING A LOOSE COVER...

There are a number of complicated fixes for loose book covers and one very simple fix. And as life's too short for complicated nonsense, let's concentrate on the easy option. This only applies to books where the cover was glued directly onto the spine of the book. If it was, but the glue has dried and worked itself loose, here's how you mend it:

Step 1. Peel any old adhesive off the spine, then apply a fresh coat of pH-neutral adhesive and leave it until it's tacky, which should take five minutes or so. While that dries, apply another coat of adhesive along the spine on the inside of the cover.

Step 2. Push the cover back onto the spine, sticking glued edge onto tacky edge, align it neatly, and rub gently for a good fit. Place a heavy weight on the face of the book overnight as the glue dries, and when you return the next morning, it'll be as good as new.

REPAIRING A BROKEN SPINE ON A HARDBACK BOOK...

Step 1. If the spine has worked itself loose, so that it now just flaps independent of the pages, cut a piece of cloth just long enough to cover the entire length of the spine, with an extra 1 cm on either side.

Step 2. Apply a layer of pH-neutral adhesive to one side of the cloth and position so that it sits cleanly over the spine when you push it into place. The extra 2 cm you cut should now sit on either side of the spine, with one part on the inside of the front cover and the other on the inside of the back cover. Push the cloth down flat and wipe away any excess glue from the cover, hinges, spine, and pages.

Step 3. Make sure the spine and hinges are properly aligned, then place the book under a heavy book or books and leave to dry overnight to complete the job.

A SPINELESS QUICK FIX

If the spine has simply worked loose but remains in place along either crease, a fresh application of glue along the spine will do the trick. The tricky bit here is reaching the spine, but this is possible by slathering a knitting needle in glue and inserting it down the spine and onto the edge of the book block. When you've applied enough glue, push the spine back onto the book block and hold until the glue takes. Place the book under a heavy object until the glue sets and the spine works as normal again.

For any other fix, or if it's a particularly precious antique book, take it to an expert and tell him to be careful.

How to... Fix a Fishing Rod

Most fishing rods are built sturdy enough to let you wrestle with giant, growling fish, yet delicate enough to crack and snap when you accidentally cast off and clatter into anything other than water. Research shows that when fishing rods break, it's usually the little O-shaped ring on the end that goes first—known as the "tip" ring. Luckily, a fractured tip ring can very easily be fixed using a combination of heat, some glue, and a replacement ring that you keep in your galoshes, or whatever it is that you fishermen wear. Once you have the parts, the fixing is straightforward.

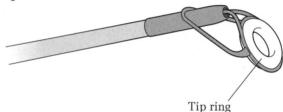

Tip ring

Step 1. Holding a cigarette lighter 2.5 cm or so away from the tip of the shaft where the ring is attached to the rod, gently heat the tip. Take care not to get too close with the flame or overheat it or you'll melt the rod itself, which is irreversible. Your aim here is, very gently, to heat and loosen the glue holding the ring in place, then pull at the ring with a small pair of pliers, or, if you have no pliers, your hand in a glove (gloved to avoid picking up an agonizing burn). With just enough heat, it should slide gently away.

Step 2. Use your lighter to heat up a stick of hot melted glue, then smear this generously over the tip of the rod and slide the replacement tip into place, making sure it lines up with the rod's guides. Allow it to set firm, which should take a matter of minutes, then feel free to cast off again, only this time taking greater care.

How to... Fix a Sluggish Skateboard*

If the wheels on your board or skates feel slow and sluggish, to the point that it might be quicker to just walk instead of roll to wherever it is you're going, you almost certainly have a problem with the bearings. These live inside the wheels and mount said wheels onto the axle, but over time they become clogged up with grime that slows them down. This grime needs to be cleaned and the bearings lubricated before they can run smoothly again. Here's how:

You should have four wheels in all. Any less and you may have the reason for your board being so sluggish.

*Or roller skates.

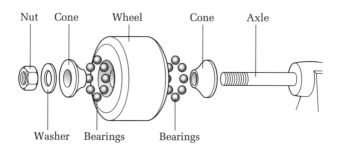

Nut   Cone   Wheel   Cone   Axle

Washer   Bearings   Bearings

Step 1. Take a wrench and remove the nut holding the wheel in place.

Step 2. Use the tip of a screwdriver to carefully pry the two sets of bearings from the center of each wheel-they should pop out with just a little effort. Count them up and keep them safe; you should have eight bearings in all.

Step 3. Stick all eight bearings in a jar of rubbing alcohol, give it a good shake, and leave them to soak for ten minutes. Remove them from the jar and dry on a cloth, rubbing off any dirt that has stubbornly remained.

Step 4. Add just a small amount of lubricating oil to each bearing—one or two drops per bearing is more than enough, but it needs to be distributed evenly over each one.

Step 5. To reattach the wheels to the axle, put both sets of bearings on the shaft first, then push the wheel down on top and it should click into place, with the bearings back in the center. Spin each wheel to make sure it runs cleanly, then reattach the nut, taking care not to overtighten it; otherwise, the wheel won't run freely and you may end up eating dirt.

Step 6. You're all done and free to catch some radical big air, or something.

How to... Replace the Tip of a Pool/Snooker Cue

Pool and snooker cue manufacturers strongly advise that when the tip of your cue becomes worn or damaged, you should have it replaced by an expert. But then they would say that. What they don't tell you is that if you know your ass from your elbow, then you're more than capable of replacing the tip yourself to a high standard, like so:

Step 1. Buy a replacement tip from any decent sports shop. You will need to buy one that is slightly larger than the "ferrule," which is the fancy way of saying the "end bit of the cue" onto which you'll stick the tip, then trim it down to size.

Step 2. Carefully remove what's left of the old or damaged tip with a razor blade, then sand the ferrule with coarse sandpaper so you're left with a rough but level surface that will take a blob of glue. Now sand the bottom of the cue tip until it's every bit as rough as the ferrule.

Step 3. Apply glue to both parts and push them together, making sure the tip's as central as possible. Hold it for a minute or two until the glue sets, then leave overnight to let it set properly.

Step 4. In the morning, or at your earliest convenience if you have more pressing matters to take care of, use a craft knife to carefully trim away any part of the tip that's overhanging so that it's in line with the cue. Wet the edges of the tip and use sandpaper to shape it to a professional finish. That's you set, so play on.

How to... Re-Grip a Tennis/Badminton Racket

A tennis racket with a ripped or ragged grip is no good at match-point at the end of a five-set epic when your palms are sweaty, your nerves frayed, and your reputation at your local tennis club on the line. It should never come to this, not if you take care of your racket.

As its name suggests, a grip needs to provide a good

solid grip. If it's frayed or faulty in any way, it needs to be replaced, either by stripping the old grip down and starting from scratch or by adding an overgrip. The latter option is a new grip that goes over the existing one and is by far the easier of the two options, and therefore the one recommended here.

Step 1. Purchase a length of replacement grip, available from any half-decent sports shop. Peel off the back and wrap the sticky side around the bottom part of the handle, pulling it taut for a secure fit.

Step 2. After completing one rotation, angle the tape slightly upwards on the shaft so that it climbs up the handle and overlaps the previous layer by 6 mm or so and complete the next rotation. Repeat this process. Make sure each rotation is as clean as possible, with no unsightly kinks or air pockets.

Step 3. Continue upward until you reach the top of the handle. To keep it securely in place, stretch a length of heavy-duty tape over your final layer of grip and you should have a solid hold once more.

How to... Re-Grip A Golf Club

When the rubbery old grips on your golf clubs begin to fray and come loose, you'll lose all purchase on your balls, as Tarby probably once said to Brucey. Your best bet is to rip off the old grip and start again. This is easy enough, providing you can be trusted to use a sharp knife.

Step 1. Rip the old grip off with a hooked Stanley knife blade (like a normal blade, but with a hooked end) or a similar model, donning thick gloves to keep your pinkies safe. If the grip is particularly old, it may break up as you rip, which will take you more time and effort to remove.

Step 2. With your gloves still on, use your thumb to rub white spirit onto the shaft to remove any grip tape left behind—it may take a while to get every last shred off, but it needs to be done or the new tape you put on won't be even.

Step 3. Completely cover the now clean shaft with double-sided sticky tape.

Step 4. Secure the club in a vise using a hand towel or, if you're impressively equipped, a rubber clamp. Either way, take the gripless shaft and place it in the vise/clamp, making sure the toe of the club is facing upward. Take the new grip, which will be long and hollow with a hole on the bottom (which will let out the white spirit when you pour the liquid into the new shaft in a minute to provide lubrication). You need to plug the small hole with your finger and pour a good glug of white spirit into the grip. Take your finger away from the hole and the white spirit will drain out, so don't take your finger off the grip. Instead, work the liquid around the inside to provide lubrication along the full length of the grip.

Step 5. Now pour a little more white spirit on the grip tape to make it slippery and also, crucially, to release the glue within the tape. Then slip the grip onto the shaft, making sure its guidelines are square with the face.

Step 6. Cut off any excess grip tape with a utility knife and clean up with white spirit to give a top-end finish. Leave to dry for at least thirty minutes before teeing off again.

How to... Adjust Bicycle Brakes: Part I

So there you are, riding along while daydreaming about cheese or that promotion you've been after, when suddenly you spot a red light. No problem, you think, applying the brakes in good time. But... oh no... they're not working and... oh shit... you'll soon be under that there bus!

Presumably you don't want this to happen to you, so you'll need to check your brakes before heading out. When bike brakes fail, most often it's a case either of the brakes being worn and consequently becoming too far away from the rim, making the brake feel loose and unresponsive, or the brake blocks might be set too close to the rim, making them feel tight and jerky (see page 196). If your problem is the former, read on...

Brake cables

Rear brake

Front brake

Step 1. Test the brake first, by pulling gently on the brake lever. The lever should pull back to the handlebars, no more than between a quarter to halfway. If it pulls any farther back, then the brake blocks (or brake pads) are worn or badly installed and so are now too far from the rim. (If the brake blocks look worn beyond repair, see pages 197–198 for instructions on how to replace.)

Step 2. To adjust the blocks by hand, turn the barrel adjuster, which looks like a very small barrel and normally sits where the cable meets the brake arm. A quick turn counterclockwise should tighten the cable and bring the brake arms closer to the wheel.

Step 3. Test the brakes again, and if the brake lever still pulls too far toward you, find the nut on the brake arm that secures the cable and loosen it with a wrench. With the nut loosened, hold the brake cable and pull on it until the brake arm (and the brake blocks) move closer to the rim of the wheel—the blocks should sit close to the rim but *should not be touching*. Also, make sure that the brake blocks come into contact with the rim only, never the tire. Once they're in position, tighten the bolt to secure the cable.

Step 4. Test the brake lever again. It should now be about right. If it needs a further tweak, turning the barrel adjuster again can fine-tune things.

Step 5. Repeat all of the above on the other brake, because you should have two, and only when you've done both can you consider yourself finished and your brakes road worthy again.

WARNING!

If you are in any doubt about your brakes, or if the brake cable appears faulty or damaged, consult an expert and have them fix it for you.

How to... Adjust Bicycle Brakes: Part II

Brake blocks that are set too close to the rim will stop the wheels on your bike from turning smoothly and, if you're really unlucky, send you hurtling over the handlebars when you pull on the brake levers. And that will hurt, so...

Step 1. Test the wheel by lifting it off the floor and spinning it by hand. If the blocks seem to rub against the rim, they're set too close and need to be loosened off.

Step 2. Locate the brake alignment screw, which should sit on each brake next to the wheel rim. Turn whichever needs turning with an Allen key until the blocks begin to move away from the rim. Spin the wheel again to test.

Step 3. If the brakes remain too close to the rim, loosen the nut that holds the brake cable in place, then loosen the cable itself by hand until the blocks start to open out and move away from the rim. When you're happy with the blocks' position, retighten the nut to hold them in place. Test the wheel by spinning it, just to be sure.

How to... Replace Worn Brake Blocks

Completely worn brake blocks will leave you hurtling down a steep hill going "agghhhhshitIdontwantto-dieaggghhhh!" as you realize you have no obvious way of stopping. The problem, you see, is that every time you apply your brakes the pads rub against the wheel rim and wear away a little, and over time they'll become less effective. Luckily, most bolt-on blocks have a helpful little "wear" line on them to indicate when they're reaching danger levels. When they wear down to that line (or they wear on one side but not the other), you'll need to replace them as follows:

Step 1. Working on one block at a time (so that you can refer to the block on the opposite side as you work), use a wrench to loosen and remove the nut holding it in place. Pull out the defective pad and insert a new one. That's the really easy bit.

Step 2. Now, by hand, position the block so that it mirrors the block on the opposite side of the wheel, making sure that when you squeeze the brake lever both blocks strike the rim squarely. The full length of each block should press against the rim when you brake, with no more than a couple of millimeters of rim showing above it. If the blocks feel stiff to move, apply a little lubricant to the whole brake arm mechanism, oiling each of its parts to encourage it along.

Step 3. To reduce the sound of squeaking and the risk of causing damage to the rim, make sure the front of the block is positioned so that it comes into contact with the rim first. You need to ensure there's about a 5 mm gap between the front of the block and the back.

Step 4. When you're happy with the positioning, tighten the retaining nut fully, checking the block stays in place until it's secure, then move onto the next block, repeating the process we've just gone over. Then do the next one on the other wheel, and then do the last one. And then stop.

How to... Patch Up a Bicycle Puncture

You could always pay an old man ten dollars to patch the hole up for you, but you'd be a fool to do so, because providing you have a puncture repair kit, the rest is pretty much idiot-proof.

Step 1. Flip the bike on its head and remove the wheel, either using the clever quick-release lever or by unscrewing the axle nuts. Use a wrench for this (rather than your hands, or you'll be there all day), and use tire levers (available from bike shops) to pry the tire from the rim, section by section, until the tire and inner tube come free together.

Step 2. Feel around the inside of the tire to check for whatever caused the puncture: a nail, a thorn, a sharp stone, etc. Remove the object, hold it up to eye level to scrutinize for no other reason than it seems the right thing to do, then discard it somewhere out of the way. Over your neighbor's wall, perhaps.

Step 3. Remove the inner tube from the tire, by hand, then locate the hole by pumping the tube back up, because it's the tube and not the tire that is punctured. When inflated, hold the inner tube under water and look for bubbles—they will give the hole's location away. Chalk a Union Jack-style cross (four lines) over the hole, then scuff over the hole with emery paper until the middle of the cross is erased. The rough surface will take a splodge of glue better at Step 4, and even though the middle of the cross has been rubbed off, the eight remaining lines of the Union Jack will still point to the center of the target.

Step 4. Apply a nice blob of glue on and around the hole, making sure it covers an area larger than the patch you'll apply, which itself should be large enough to completely cover the hole. When the glue has partially dried but still feels tacky, apply another blob to the underside of the patch, place over the hole, and push down firmly for a couple of minutes.

Step 5. Make a final check for any sharp objects that may still be inside the tire so you don't leave anything in that may cause another puncture. Then pump up the inner tube just enough to give it some shape, before reinserting the inner tube, valve first. Make sure the valve is straight and that you avoid any twists or kinks in the inner tube.

Step 6. Work the outer tire back over the wheel rim, using your fingers. Pump a little more air in to check the tube isn't caught between the rim and the tire, then reattach the wheel and pump up fully. Cycle away, pulling a celebratory "wheelie," if you're that way inclined.

AN EMERGENCY ALTERNATIVE

Imagine this scenario, if you will. The tire is pancake flat and you have no repair kit with which to bring it back to life. And it's a really long walk home lugging this shabby bike, too. Panic not, for help could be at hand, providing you can get your hands on some grass. (Horticultural grass, obviously.)

Step 1. Remove the deflated tube from your wheel, as outlined above, and keep it safe. Put it in your pocket, maybe.

Step 2. Stuff grass into the tire, molding it around the circumference. This will take time, particularly if you're to spread the grass evenly around the tire. When done, the grass will provide the cushioning of an inflated inner tube.

Step 3. Replace the tire, shake your head, and ask yourself how it came to this, then cycle off into the distance on your new comedy wheel. Go slowly to avoid damaging the rim and perform a proper repair once you're safely home.

How to... Repair a Scratched Car

At a guess, some jerk probably keyed it, or clumsily clanked their shopping cart along your bodywork at the supermarket. Yes, you have every right to be livid. A good beating is all "their sort" are fit for, etc. and so on.

In this situation, however, how the scratch came about matters less than finding a simple fix. And finding that fix depends on the depth of the gouge.

A deep scratch on a car can invite corrosion if it goes first through the paint, then through the primer, and finally down into the metal. If you inspect the scratch and see metallic grey at the bottom, cry "blast and botheration!" or "cock and balls!" and then call an expert before it starts to corrode. However, if you inspect the scratch and see there's still color at the bottom, you can fix it yourself. Like so:

Step 1. Clean the affected area well with soapy water and leave it to dry completely. When it's bone dry, take a shoe polish of a contrasting color to the car's paint and rub it over the scratch or scratches. This makes no sense, you might think, but it will shortly...

Step 2. Sand the scratch using a wet-dry sandpaper, bought from an auto repair type outlet—2000-grit is usually sufficient. Dip the paper in cold water to improve purchase and sand the scratch *very, very gently indeed*, going in one direction rather than back and forth, and using light, short strokes. As soon as the shoe polish has gone, this will indicate that you've reached the level of the scratch (see, told you it would make sense), at which point you should stop sanding.

Step 3. Apply a rubbing compound—ask the man behind the counter as it's sold under a more snappy name in automobile shops—to a soft, clean cloth and polish out the sanding scratches you'll have left, moving in a nice, steady circular motion.

Step 4. To finish, lightly buff with a new, soft clean cloth to remove the last of the compound, then apply a layer of car wax to protect from the elements and you should be done, at least until the next time some idiot ruins your paint job. And they will.

How to... Fix a Defective Windshield Wiper

You could easily dismiss the odd crack on a windshield wiper blade as a trifling matter, an insignificance that shouldn't cause you to lose any sleep. But as you should have guessed this far into the book, you'd be wrong.

At best, a cracked wiper will annoy you every time you use it. At worst, the cracks will cause smearing on your windshield, so you won't be able to see where you're driving and may end up in a ditch. That would be terrible, so act fast to fix it at the first sign of smearing.

Step 1. Turn the engine off and assess the damage to each blade, including the wiper on the back windshield and any you may have on your headlights. If you spot any cracks, measure the length of the blades and buy replacements that match exactly. Most modern blades are sold ready-fitted to their metal mountings, which is preferable as they're easier to fix than replacing the rubber section alone, which can be a right fiddle.

Step 2. Lay the replacement blades on the bonnet, positioned beneath the defective blades for reference. Lift the wiper arm away from the screen until it locks in a vertical position, so blade and arm sit in a T position.

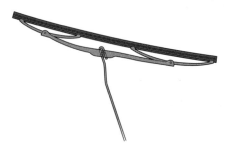

Step 3. Unclip or unfasten the old blade, either by hand or using a screwdriver, then release the blade and place it somewhere over there. Now attach the replacement blade by reversing the above. Clip it securely into place, then lower the blade back into place, wet the screen, and test to make sure it wipes as it should. If it doesn't, double-check that it's secured and positioned as it should be.

How to... Fix a Flat Tire

Otherwise known as How to Change a Spare Tire Rather Than Call a Man From the AAA Who'll Take an Age to Arrive and Charge You a Large Amount of Cash for the Honor. It's easy enough, you see, albeit quite involved.

Step 1. When you realize you have a flat, slow down to pensioner pace (5 mph or so) to minimize damage to the wheel and pull over to a safe place. Turn off the engine, flick the hazard lights on, and apply the handbrake. If it's a manual car, put it in reverse, if automatic; select "P" for "park."

Step 2. Remove any luggage and passengers to lighten the load and put down a warning triangle, if you're one of the few people who actually owns one, to encourage other drivers to give you a wide berth.

Step 3. Locate your spare tire (it's normally in the trunk and needs to be fully inflated) and the essential tools you need—a wheel brace and jack, plus your car's handbook. Leave the wheel grounded for now, but pry off the wheel trim—either with a flat-bladed screwdriver or, in an emergency, a sturdy key.

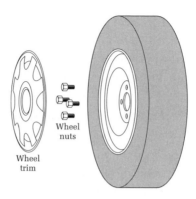

Wheel
nuts

Wheel
trim

Step 4. Use the brace to give the wheel nuts a half turn counterclockwise, just enough to loosen them, unscrewing them diagonally to keep the wheel stable and balanced—so unscrew one, then unscrew the one diagonal to it. If the nuts are particularly stiff, coat them with a little oil and leave for a few minutes.

Step 5. Your handbook should suggest the safest, sturdiest lifting point on the car to extract the damaged wheel. Refer to the book and, using your jack, raise the car up so the body is elevated but the damaged wheel still touches the ground, then push the spare wheel under the body, so if the car slips off the jack the tire will at least cushion the blow. Keep jacking the car up until the flat wheel is just clear of the road, then unscrew the nuts in diagonal pairs, remove and keep them safe.

Step 6. Remove the wheel, which will be heavy and coated in oil and bits of road kill. Place it under the raised sill of the car for cushioning, having obviously removed the spare tire first. Stick the good tire onto the hub, the right way round, and fit the nuts on in diagonal formation again, tightening with your fingers for now. Use the jack to lower the car until the tire just touches the ground, then tighten the nuts properly and refit the wheel trim.

Step 7. Shove the damaged tire in the trunk, lower the car fully, and remove the jack. Refill the car with bags and people, then mirror, signal, and maneuver on your way. Balls, you've left your warning triangle on the road.

WARNING!

It is vital to check your spare tire as carefully as those in day-to-day use and to be prepared for changing a tire, which you may need to do in fairly difficult locations. Familiarize yourself with the location of the car jack, the spare tire, and the wheel-locking nut tool before you need to use them. Ensure you have a wheel brace as well as an inflated spare tire, and know the location of your wheel-locking nut if your car has one.

If you have a mini spare rather than full size, these are designed to save space and get you home, but not to be driven on for long periods. Many of the space savers can not be used at speeds over 50 mph; consult your space saver wheel or vehicle handbook for specific details.